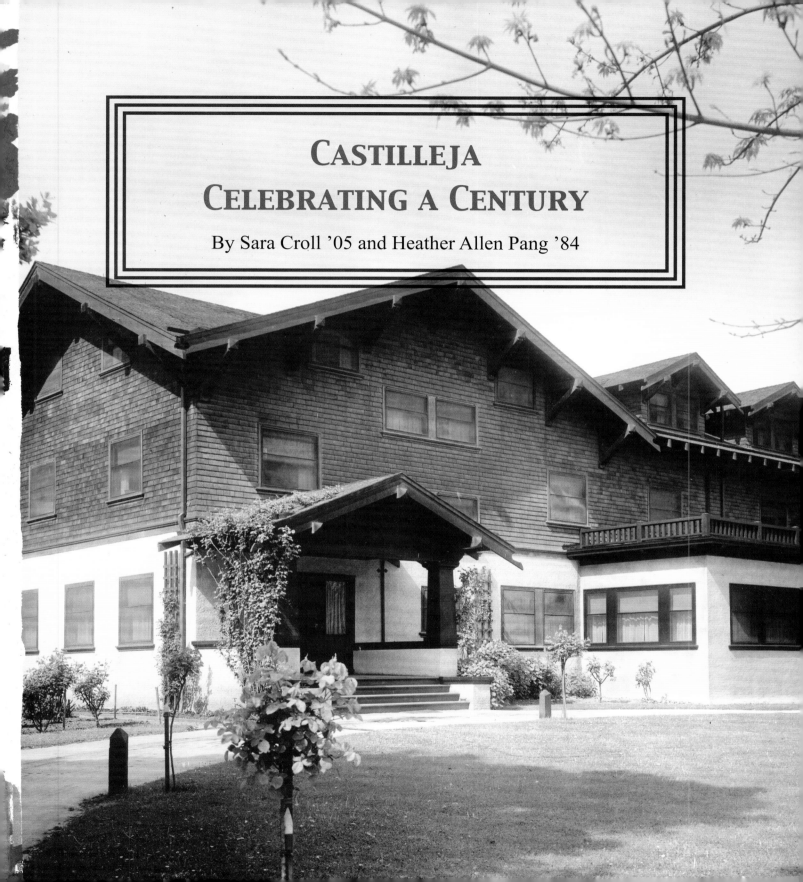

CASTILLEJA
CELEBRATING A CENTURY

By Sara Croll '05 and Heather Allen Pang '84

ISBN: 0-9794860-0-9

Published by Castilleja School
1310 Bryant Street
Palo Alto, California 94301

Telephone: 650.328.3160
Fax: 650.326.8036

http://www.castilleja.org

Printed by Capital Offset Company Inc.
Concord, New Hampshire

"In order to instill...a sense of pride in our school and a sense of commitment to our community, we must understand what has come before us; we must tell and retell the Castilleja story."
—Anjelika Deogirikar '00

CONTENTS

Castilleja School
1907-2007

This Centennial history is dedicated to Castilleja's classroom teachers, past and present. We honor and celebrate them for their excellence in teaching, their dedication to the school, and their commitment to generations of Castilleja alumnae and students.

FROM THE HEAD

This extensively researched written history of Castilleja is both a window and a mirror. On the eve of our Centennial year, *Castilleja: Celebrating a Century* allows us to understand and reflect upon the extraordinary foundation and enduring commitment to excellence that have sustained this institution for 100 years.

Thousands of girls, and a few little boys, have passed through our doors since the first 68 students began their Castilleja education in August of 1907. Intelligent, strong, good-hearted women in all walks of life sustain Castilleja's proud legacy. Alumnae reflect the strength and diversity of our school through their life choices and contributions to making the world around them—whether on the Circle or beyond—a better place.

Just leafing through these pages is a wonderful reminder of how, through the decades, Castilleja women have taken to heart the adage "to whom much is given, much is expected." Today's students follow the example of generations of alumnae in adhering to our five Cs—courtesy, conscience, charity, courage, and character—throughout their lives.

We have a new tradition, one that began last year and shall continue. On the first day of school, every new student is inducted into the Castilleja Alumnae Association. She receives a gold Castilleja pin for the knot of her class tie, signifying her new status as an alumna of Castilleja. This year, in recognition of the extraordinary construction projects, all students received a second pin, a small shovel, to symbolize our collective "digging in" as we build together the next 100 years—a second century of excellence.

The story of Castilleja's perseverance and dedication in meeting challenges, overcoming obstacles, and embracing change reminds us of our debt to the past, and our obligation to the future. We build Castilleja's future boldly and with confidence on a solid foundation. Together, we shall keep our school strong and vital. Castilleja is truly a place of Women Learning, Women Leading.

Joan Lonergan

The ceremony for laying the cornerstone of the Recitation Hall–now known as the Gunn Family Administration Building–took place in 1910, when Castilleja moved to its current site. Mary Lockey stands to the left with David Starr Jordan. Martha Faull '20 places an object in the time capsule. The capsule was uncovered in the recent renovation of the building and replaced alongside a new one in 2003.

Chapter One
STARTING A SCHOOL

"Miss Lockey announces the opening of her school in Palo Alto on the 19th of August, at 1121 Bryant Street. The School...will be known as Castilleja."[1]

CASTILLEJA

The school name shared by both Castilleja Hall and Castilleja School comes from the botanical name of the flower Indian Paintbrush. David Starr Jordan suggested the name for the school because he admired the botanist Domingo Castillejo, for whom the flower was named.

Arriving in Palo Alto on the Southern Pacific Railroad from San Francisco in 1907, visitors walked into a small downtown on University Avenue. To the west, the sprawling campus of the recently established Stanford University reached out toward the hills; to the south, a growing residential community of brown-shingle, Craftsman-style homes dotted the landscape toward Embarcadero Road. At the edge of this budding university town, Mary Ishbel Lockey found a home for her new school. She wished to educate women, and her mentor, Stanford President David Starr Jordan, encouraged her to start a school in Palo Alto that would prepare girls for Stanford. She supplied the hard work and daily dedication; he the advice and experience. In the fall of 1907, Miss Lockey opened Castilleja School with 14 teachers and 68 day and resident pupils. Girls were enrolled in kindergarten through twelfth grade; the grammar school was coed. Castilleja flourished, and in 1910 the school moved from a small rented

Top: The original Castilleja site at 1121 Bryant Street.

Oval: Miss Lockey in 1910 waits to move into the new school.

building that had previously housed at least two other schools to its own five-acre campus where it remains today. So great was Dr. Jordan's faith in Miss Lockey, and so impressive was her success, that he remarked in a 1910 address to the school that his "implicit confidence in Miss Lockey" was such that he "would not hesitate to turn over the management of Stanford [to her], were it necessary."[2] One hundred years after its founding, Castilleja School remains the enduring legacy of its dynamic founder. Despite significant changes over its first century, the school has remained true to the core of Miss Lockey's mission to give each young women an "educated heart."[3]

Mary Ishbel Lockey was born in Helena, Montana, on June 21, 1872. After graduating from high school, she spent a year at the Froebel-Pestalozzi Schule in Berlin, Germany, and then began her teacher training at the Normal School in Helena before transferring to Stanford University and graduating in 1902. At Stanford, she was one of the founders of the Alpha Phi sorority; later she was retroactively elected a charter member of the new Stanford Phi Beta Kappa chapter. Her career in education began at the Miss Harker–Miss Hughes School in Palo Alto, and she also taught at Palo Alto High School. These experiences gave her the skills and confidence to found Castilleja and become its first Principal. She also taught English in Castilleja's high school during the early years. The Lockey family supported her in her education and, later, in her career. Her brother Richard had come to Stanford when she did, and their mother accompanied them to

California. Their father had made his fortune in the mining boom in Montana and moved from his established law practice into politics. The Lockey family provided the financial resources needed to establish Castilleja by buying stock in the school.

Mary Lockey also had help from Dr. Jordan, who, after her graduation from Stanford, continued to mentor her as her career in education progressed. His enthusiasm for preparing girls for Stanford followed a model common in the Progressive Era. Since the 1880s, advocates of women's education had complained about the inferior early schooling of entering college freshmen and had worked for the creation of girls' schools that would prepare girls for college. The Dana Hall School was founded in 1881 by two Wellesley faculty members at the request of the college's president, and the Baldwin School was founded in 1888 to prepare girls for Bryn Mawr.[4] On the West Coast, the need was even more acute, and schools for boys and girls sprang up in the early twentieth century to ensure that western students would be as qualified for college as their eastern counterparts. In southern

Top: Students ride in a horse-drawn carriage during the 1908-09 school year.

Oval: Miss Elizabeth G. Hughes taught science, mathematics, and Bible at Castilleja and served as Associate Principal for many years.

California, Harvard School for Boys, founded in 1900, and Westlake School for Girls, founded in 1904, are prominent examples of this new enthusiasm for California college preparatory schools.[5]

But despite their own enthusiasm, when pioneers of women's education established the first girls' schools in the 1840s, they were attacked for the supposed harm serious study and concentrated thought would do to a girl's mind and body. Critics charged that women were not capable of mastering difficult subjects like algebra and history, and that education would make them unfit for motherhood. Although these debates about women's education had begun to quiet down by the early twentieth century, educating girls for college was still a progressive project, and not a little bit radical. The late nineteenth century had witnessed the expansion of women's education, but the purpose and content of that education remained controversial.

Like many girls' high schools in the early twentieth century, Castilleja tried to please both those who argued for teaching girls to be good mothers and housewives and those who believed that girls should have the same strong, classical curriculum that boys needed to go to college. From the beginning, Castilleja truly was a college preparatory school, although "a general course [was] arranged for pupils not desiring to enter College."[6] For all the girls, Miss Lockey and her staff aimed to provide "an education that is broad, not merely academic."[7] The school chose this dual system as a way of maintaining the support of the proponents of both perspectives on women's education. It also reassured parents that their daughters would not be "overeducated" and therefore unfit for marriage. This was a common solution for girls' schools of the era.[8] This dualism also allowed girls to gain both sets of skills, academic and domestic. Castilleja's early catalogues point out that each student's program could be arranged to suit any particular needs. They stress that "in every case an effort will be made to develop systematic and scholarly habits of thought"[9] and also that "particular attention is given to training in social customs, grace of manner, and refinement of speech."[10]

In the high school, girls studied English, Latin, German, and French, history (ancient, medieval and modern, English, and American);

"graduates of Castilleja were admitted without examination to Stanford"

Graduating seniors in 1910 predict their futures in the Senior Class Prophecy. Emma Laumeister is a suffragette, hoping to win the vote for California's women; Olive Smith is a model mother; and Beth Munger is a nurse.

mathematics (algebra and geometry); and science (zoology and physiology). The college preparatory program evidently was successful; from the second year of operation, graduates of Castilleja were admitted without examination to Stanford "when their work [was] recommended by the principal and teachers."[11] This list of colleges grew to include the University of California, Wellesley, Smith, Vassar, Mills, Mount Holyoke, and Wells.

In addition to these academic subjects, "hygiene" class included gymnasium work, walking and climbing, first aid, and a period of laboratory work and recitation. "Domestic Science" and "Domestic Art" were both required for the college preparatory program, as were art and music. Domestic Science and Domestic Art gave the girls "a practical and scientific knowledge of household economics, with a view to developing and guiding what should be their natural tastes and tendencies."[12] The girls learned to cook, because, as one alumna remembered, Miss Lockey did not want any newlywed Castilleja bride embarrassed by serving her husband hard biscuits. These courses took place in the Domestic Science Bungalow,

which doubled as Miss Lockey's residence and was "built and furnished as a model cottage where girls may learn thoroughly and practically the art of home-making and home-keeping."[13]

Lessons on domesticity were not limited to the classroom. For the residence students, every part of their day was an opportunity for training in womanly arts and behavior. Dancing classes were a regular evening activity on Friday or Saturday, and students were encouraged to read, sing, or talk around the open fire after dinner. In every way, Castilleja assured prospective parents that "the spirit of family [was] being preserved as far as possible."[14] Castilleja promoted its dormitory program with an emphasis on the health and happiness provided to resident students: "It will be the aim to make the home-life simple, healthful, and happy, and to provide suitable social recreation. Only such rules as exist in every well-regulated family will be insisted upon, but proper chaperonage will always be provided. In recognition of the fact that health is the first condition of vigorous mental life, special care will be taken of the physical condition of the pupils."[15] Girls were required to keep their own rooms clean for

Top: The 1910-11 French class gets a cultural experience as they sample French food.

Oval: Russell and Sigurd Varian were students at Castilleja. Although, as boys, they could not continue into high school, several of their relatives are graduates. Susan Varian Hammond '69, Sidney Varian Scott '84, Holly Varian Zuklie '86, and Claire Varian '96 are all related to Russell and Sigurd Varian.

Top left: Young students enjoy Thanksgiving, one of the many occasions for dressing up in costume. Hortense Berry, '13, is the girl in this 1907 picture.

Top right: This man is moving Miss Lockey's belongings from the old campus to the new campus on August 15, 1910.

Oval: Miss Sterns was Castilleja's beloved longtime Housemother.

A Castilleja School stock certificate from 1910

inspection, spend an hour on Sundays mending their own clothes, and assist the teachers "in their At Home, the first Thursday of the month."[16] Miss Lockey and her staff intended to provide training in home life that was equal or superior to what the girls would have experienced in their own homes.

Miss Lockey brought well-educated women to the faculty to help achieve a curriculum that was cultured and refined while also academically rigorous. More than half of the instructors in the Preparatory Department or High School had college degrees, and a few had earned their Master's. In addition to the teachers, Miss Lockey had two women help her

administer Castilleja. The Assistant Principal was Miss Elizabeth G. Hughes, one of the founding heads of the Miss Harker–Miss Hughes School where Miss Lockey had taught. Miss Florence Curry Sterns served as the first Housemother.

While the majority of the students at every grade came from Palo Alto, the school also drew from around the San Francisco Bay Area, including Sausalito, Menlo Park, San Francisco, Woodside, Oakland, and Berkeley, as well as other western states, including Washington, Montana, and Arizona. Tuition and board for a resident student cost $750 a year; tuition for a day student was $150 in the first year. Optional music lessons, laboratory fees, special uniforms, books, art materials, and chaperoning were additional.

Castilleja built its reputation primarily on the high school and excellent college preparatory program, but the grammar school included both girls and boys and proved popular with Palo Alto residents. The course of study for the primary, intermediate, and grammar grades included reading, language, arithmetic, science, spelling, drawing, music, physical training, history, geography, physiology, and grammar. Yet while

The Residence from Bryant Street on August 15, 1910,
just before the school moved onto the campus.

The Sixth C: Construction

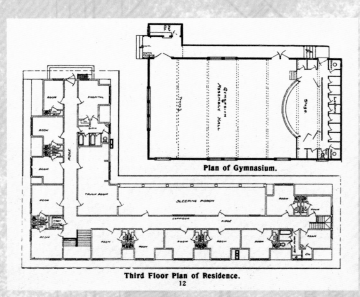

Plan of Gymnasium.

Third Floor Plan of Residence.
12

Miss Lockey's plans for the new campus in 1910 included a dormitory, a recitation building, a domestic science building, and a gymnasium. The estimated cost of this construction was $50,000. Having secured the services of local planner and contractor Gustav Laumeister, Miss Lockey proceeded to shape the school around the edges of the block in order to create a circle in the center. When she advertised the school in the 1910-11 catalogue, she highlighted the new features and their benefits to students: "These plans are especially adapted to the school and the climate, and are most attractive and practical. The buildings are strongly built and braced and have excellent fire protection; the plumbing and the heating plant are of the latest and most approved systems. Though the school lies just beyond the town limits, there is connection with the Palo Alto sewer...The sleeping porch is one of the most attractive features of the building; it is situated on the third floor, ...has a southern exposure, a roof, and protection from drafts and driving storms. Here, if desired, girls may sleep out of doors all winter...The spacious living rooms are especially planned for entertaining and for comfort. Small round tables are a feature of the beautiful, cheery dining room...Particular attention has been paid to the lighting of all the buildings, and in the Recitation Hall every room has east or south sun." Although the level of detail may sound strange to modern readers, the connections between physical settings and educational goals were essential to the early-twentieth-century advocates of reform who believed there was a connection between educational achievement and physical surroundings. Such thinking was one of the reasons Miss Lockey was as proud of her campus outside as she was of it inside: "Splendid live oak trees beautify the property, producing a park-like effect, and lawns, fruit trees, and gardens are already in a state of advanced growth and bloom possible only in a climate like that of California." Miss Lockey's careful and thoughtful design for the school in its first major construction was so strong that basic elements of her plan are still recognizable today.

the classroom curriculum appears rigorous and academic, the photo albums of the era tell more of the story. Children dressed in elaborate costumes for Thanksgiving, Halloween, and every possible dramatic occasion. Some enterprising children once posed all of their dolls and bears on the steps of the school for a photographer. The children often played on the grounds of the school, with sports and outdoor play a regular part of the school day.

In the school's first year, Miss Lockey started with only 68 students in kindergarten through the twelfth grade. In fewer than five years, the school had not only settled into its own campus but also boasted a student body of more than 125 day and boarding students and a staff of over 20 teachers and administrators. It did not take long for the school to outgrow the rented site at 1121 Bryant Street. In 1910, Miss Lockey purchased the current site of the school, a block bounded by Bryant, Melville, Kellogg, and Emerson Streets with an unobstructed view across the meadows to the foothills. With the acquisition of this property for $20,000 from Alfred Seale, father of Marion Seale '22 and Barbara Seale '24, the school

began the first of many large-scale building programs. The four-and-a-half-acre block soon held the Residence, including the popular sleeping porch on the third floor, Recitation Hall, the gymnasium /auditorium, the Domestic Science Bungalow, and the outdoor playing fields.

The planning and construction of a new campus allowed Miss Lockey to create a school that took advantage of the mild climate. It perfectly suited her vision for girls' education: "These plans are especially adapted to the school and the climate, and are most attractive and practical. The buildings…are grouped and the grounds arranged so that the pupils may practically live out of doors."[17] This focus on healthy outdoor activities remained a selling point in every admissions publication until the Residence program ended.

The first buildings on the

Top: Three students leave for home at the end of the 1910-11 school year.

Oval: Melinda Enke '12 studies in a wheelbarrow as she enjoys the California weather in 1911.

"the finest private school on the Pacific Coast"

new property were open for the 1910-11 school year. Thanks to the efficient work of architect and builder Gustav Laumeister, some of the buildings were actually open a few weeks early so that the staff could begin moving in. Although it took several years to complete the plan, the basic layout of the campus, featuring a large circular lawn (our beloved Circle), was clear in that first year. Miss Lockey recalled that the landscaping itself was something of a trial for the school. "The gravel we had bought for the drive-ways was lost somewhere along the railroad track! But finally the grass was planted on the big Circle, and we used to cut assemblies short while Principal, teachers, and pupils pulled the big weeds." Later she hired some neighborhood boys to weed for 25 cents an hour, and Miss Lockey was pleased to note that many of those young men turned out quite well, as "evidently digging weeds was good for them intellectually, as well as physically."[18] She would often look back fondly on this formative period for the campus when she shaped the foundations of the buildings, the grounds, and the school itself.

On July 28, 1910, under the headline "All Roads Lead to Palo Alto," the *Palo Alto Times* reported the opening of the four new structures constituting "the finest private school on the Pacific Coast" at the new location on the 1300 block of Bryant Street. In its first three years, Castilleja had become an established institution in Palo Alto and was well on its way to earning this lofty praise. Miss Lockey's purchase of the current school property made it possible to craft the physical setting to fit her vision of the ideal campus. With Castilleja's future secure, the students and the faculty were ready to push forward with grand plans and hard work and to mold the school with the ideals and traditions that would serve it well over the following century.

Eleanor Fillebrown, Allan Black, and Dorothy Richards read a newspaper together in 1910.

A Castilleja student tutors at St. Elizabeth Seton School in Palo Alto as part of the Community Service program in 2004.

COMMUNITY SERVICE

"We are educating human beings and we owe it to our students to work with questions of human values, because those are the big issues when they are out there in the world."
—Jim McManus

Miss Lockey said, "Training in social service is of equal importance with that in any other field." In the 1920s, students supported the Stanford Home for Convalescent Children, the Red Cross, the European Relief Council, and French orphans. Under Miss Espinosa, students continued to focus on "service and responsibility." During World War II, students and faculty joined the Red Cross and studied first aid. Service continued in the 1950s and 1960s; the Senior Fair raised money for the Stanford Convalescent Home, and the 8th grade sent school supplies to children in Mississippi. By the 1980s, Amnesty International, the Ecumenical Hunger Program, and Spanish Service Club continued, but the school did not have a service program. In 1992, history teacher Karen Tobey reinvigorated the community service concept, and a 60-hour requirement was instituted. Under the direction of Mrs. Tobey, the program focused on developing opportunities for all students, highlighted by the annual Community Service Day. In 2006, in preparation for the Centennial celebration, the Community Service Committee replaced the hours requirement with a written reflection on service "to motivate students to serve for inherent, rather than external, rewards." Mrs. Tobey said, "As Castilleja celebrates its Centennial, we will see students more involved in global service projects, but we will also sustain our firm commitment to meeting needs within the local community."

Top: Students clean a park on Community Service Day, October 30, 1996.

Center: Chelsea Waite '07 and Rekha Arulanantham '07 pull non-native plants in 2003.

Bottom left: Students pack Thanksgiving boxes in 1935.

Below: A 1942 cartoon reminds students to bring toys for the Stanford Convalescent Home.

Bottom right: Students build the Golden Gate Bridge for the 1993 Second Harvest Food Bank drive.

UNIFORM

"It is expected that every girl will have all the required articles of uniform and that her belongings will be clearly marked. Girls are not permitted to wear 'bee-hive' or exaggerated 'hair-dos,' or makeup, when in uniform."
—Castilleja Student Handbook, *early 1960s*

Top right: Ann-Marie McMillan '92 in 1992.

Center right: Jane Hampton '21 and Ruth Vredenbugh '21 show awards on Class Day.

Below: A 1943 cartoon by Jo Glasson '43

Bottom left: Holly Varian '86 and Nancy Niland '86

Bottom center: Students wear their ties differently in 1929

Bottom right: Kim Flomenhoft '94 in the library in 1991

One of the oldest traditions at Castilleja is the student uniform. Miss Lockey established the white middies and navy pleated skirts as the basic elements of dress. Colored class ties were part of the early uniform. Early students had blue or white crepe dinner dresses! Makeup was not permitted until the 1940s, when lipstick was allowed after school. In the late 1960s, Miss Espinosa had the students vote: the result was three different uniforms, the Spring Uniform (also worn from September through Thanksgiving), the Winter Uniform, and the Dress Uniform. The light blue skirt is the one students still wear today. For a short time, the middy blouse was replaced by a "perma-press" overblouse. Miss Espinosa reported that one of the factors leading to the change was the "outdating of ironing." The uniform stayed the same through the 1980s, although without the seasonal restrictions, and the first pants were added. Under Mr. Milnor, white and red Castilleja polo shirts were added, and it was a short step from there to the current rules, allowing white and navy polos, red Castilleja polos, any collared white shirt, and navy cotton pants. The blue skirts, usually with boxers underneath, are still popular, and on dress-white days, it is easy to see the strong Castilleja traditions and the pride of the girls who wear the uniform.

Zara Saranon'12 and Lauren Barbarand'12 in 2005

Young students work diligently in their classroom during the 1916-17 academic year. Although most students were girls, boys attended in the lower grades.

Chapter Two
GROWING AND PROSPERING

"Castilleja School has the unusual advantage of both town and country life. It is situated in the best residence portion of Palo Alto, one block from the car line, but the buildings are so placed that one gets from them an unbroken view of the beautiful and fertile Santa Clara Valley.... Numberless live oaks and white oaks give from the upper windows the effect of a primeval forest, and from the earliest rains in the fall till the close of the school, the poppy-strewn fields and meadows are a constant source of inspiration."[1]

Castilleja was sitting pretty in more ways than one. Castilleja viewbooks boasted that "government records, carefully tabulated, show Palo Alto to be in the center of one of the three 'perfect climate belts' in the world. Of the other two, one is in the Canary Islands, the other in Africa."[2] But Castilleja's "situation" was just as perfect in the metaphorical sense. Having outlasted those challenging first years when many ventures fail, Castilleja's future appeared secure. The school owned the campus, and enrollment rose each year. In this early period, Mary Lockey would add many elements that still define Castilleja today.

Physically, the campus began to assume a look that is still familiar. The Chapel and swimming

CASTILLEJA PIN

The 1925-26 school catalog explains the pin: "In order to encourage an active interest in the ideals of Castilleja, the school pin is given to each new Upper School girl at the end of the first month. The privilege of wearing the pin indicates satisfactory citizenship on the part of the girl; that is, she has shown herself to be a desirable member of the school community."

Top: Students swim in the pool during the 1926-27 school year.

Center: The cover of the 1914 Indian Paintbrush, *the first yearbook published at Castilleja, showcased the C logo. Like many yearbooks of the time, early issues of the* Paintbrush *combined the literary magazine with a chronicle of the events of the year.*

"She did not wish her students to be 'foolishly afraid,' screaming 'at the sight of a caterpillar or spider or mouse'"

pool were first built in this era and remain in essentially the same places today. The school also built a science lab, the Orchard House, a gymnasium/auditorium, and a grill for the school's many outdoor luncheons.

While Castilleja's physical layout assumed a more recognizable form, other Castilleja traditions took shape. Miss Lockey initiated Arbor Day as a Castilleja holiday. In 1914, Castilleja published its first yearbook, titled *Indian Paintbrush* in a nod to the Castilleja flower. Junior-Senior Banquet and the "ringing" tradition started during this period, and 1932 saw the first Christmas Pageant.

Miss Lockey chose the "five Cs:" Courtesy, Charity, Courage, Conscience, and Character. While the five Cs are timeless and set a tone for the school that still resonates with staff and students, Miss Lockey's choices also reflected her values, which were typical of the period. In her 1930 speech, "Traditions and History," Miss Lockey explained her choices for those five "splendid words beginning with C"[3]. She felt that courtesy, "to do and say the kindest thing in the kindest way," should be extended to all people.[4] She noted that Castilleja was able to attract and retain superior staff because the girls were polite and well behaved, with the desired "low, gentle voices."[5] Courtesy also extended to respectful and attentive Chapel behavior.

She wanted her girls to possess both physical and moral courage. She did not wish her students to be "foolishly afraid," screaming "at the sight of a caterpillar or spider or mouse" or being "afraid of the dark."[6] She also, however, reminded her girls not to "be foolish in another way…remember there may be danger when you are not afraid."[7] She defined moral courage as the ability to "say 'No' when urged to do the wrong thing," and to do "what is right, even if it is not the popular side."[8] She saw courage in "really and truly serv[ing] " in student leadership positions as well as not taking "corrections as a personal matter."[9]

Miss Lockey noted that charity, which she

Students work on the Lower School Study Porch as they enjoy the spring weather in 1927.

Miss Armour poses with her kindergarten Montessori class in 1919. They patriotically wave flags to support their country and celebrate the end of the Great War even as they wear masks in an attempt to protect themselves from the deadly influenza pandemic.

defined as "love for others, charity for others not so fortunate as ourselves," was a "big part of Castilleja School life."[10] And she felt that conscience, that "small voice which does not allow us to do a dishonest or dishonorable thing," should stop students from academic dishonesty.[11]

Finally, she felt that all these attributes "unite in the word Character,"[12] and she wrote that "these 'Cs' form an arch, the keystone of which is Character."[13] The success of the five Cs is clear in a parent's letter to Miss Lockey: "I feel indebted to you for what you have done for Shelly. She has received an impetus toward fine living at Castilleja which I am sure she would have missed in any other local school… Her mind and character have developed beautifully, and she has made friends with lovely girls."[14] Mary Lockey's hopes for the five Cs had come to pass–her students had internalized these five ideals and were better for it.

The Cs were immortalized by Viola Hymen Elsbach, class of 1925, in the painting of the five Cs surrounded by the paintbrush flower which still hangs in the Administration Building. Character, as Mary Lockey intended, is the keystone of the arch in the painting.

While the set of five seems absolute today, there was a time when the five Cs were far from concrete. Miss Lockey also considered "co-operation," "cheerfulness," "citizenship," "consideration," and "concentration" as well as the more awkward "control of self," "clothes–appropriate," and "carefulness in speech."[15] She was probably wise to omit the latter set, although the tradition of brainstorming a "sixth C" to supplement the five continues today. Such traditions gave the school its individual tone and color, but Castilleja did not forget its academic purpose "to train girls in right mental habits."[16] In some subjects, however, there was simply less to learn than there is today. In recent years, eighth and eleventh grade American history classes at Castilleja have found it nearly impossible to make it through to the modern day. In contrast, 1915-16's eighth grade history class "completed the study of the book" by early April, having "brought the work up to the present time."[17] They then focused on current events, writing papers on the recently completed Panama Canal.[18]

> "Castilleja did not forget its academic purpose 'to train girls in right mental habits.'"

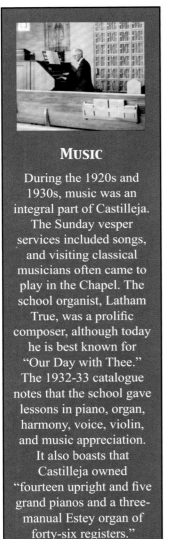

MUSIC

During the 1920s and 1930s, music was an integral part of Castilleja. The Sunday vesper services included songs, and visiting classical musicians often came to play in the Chapel. The school organist, Latham True, was a prolific composer, although today he is best known for "Our Day with Thee." The 1932-33 catalogue notes that the school gave lessons in piano, organ, harmony, voice, violin, and music appreciation. It also boasts that Castilleja owned "fourteen upright and five grand pianos and a three-manual Estey organ of forty-six registers."

Top: Florence Kent, '20, studies on the porch with Mary Thomas, '17.

Oval: Viola Russ '24 with her crabs after the 1920 Alum Rock picnic.

In a 1932 letter sent home to parents of day students, the school gave suggestions for efficient and effective studying: "Definite hours for work, kept regularly every day, are a great help, if not an absolute necessity, for satisfactory progress. A short time before dinner and two or two and a half hours after the meal should take care of the usual work. Every girl should have a quiet, comfortable place in which to work, away from the conversation and distraction of the rest of the family. She should have a desk or table large enough to accommodate her books and papers, a straight chair which is rightly proportioned for her, and a reading light."[19] The letter also stressed the importance of "good ventilation" and a learning environment of "about 68" degrees.[20] The note cautioned against the radio, phone calls, and parties on school nights, saying, "we earnestly advise against the interruption of the regular routine of work from Monday to Friday for any diversion beyond that found in physical exercise. Whatever social life is necessary for a high school girl should be confined to the week-end, and even then it should not be so strenuous that it brings her back to school on Monday exhausted

in mind and body."[21]

Although the school encouraged structure in academic focus and discouraged endless outside parties, students were having plenty of fun. Castilleja was ever intellectually demanding, but Miss Lockey intended it to consume the lives of its girls in a more total way: "It is the purpose of the Principal and her assistants to make Castilleja the center of the social life of both resident and day pupils. To that end a certain number of 'good times' which cannot interfere with the conscientious carrying-on of regular studies are scheduled for each term."[22] The students had one formal class party each semester for each grade, but they also enjoyed wacky events such as the annual picnic at Alum Rock, the Junior-Senior Banquet, and the Jolly-Up, an evening of "comical costumes," "impromptu music," and dancing that the residence girls put on to "the great amusement of teachers and day-pupils."[23]

Much of the students' entertainment came from enjoying physical activities in the great outdoors. "Castilleja School has always fostered out-of-door life for its pupils, believing that it is essential for the physical development of girls;

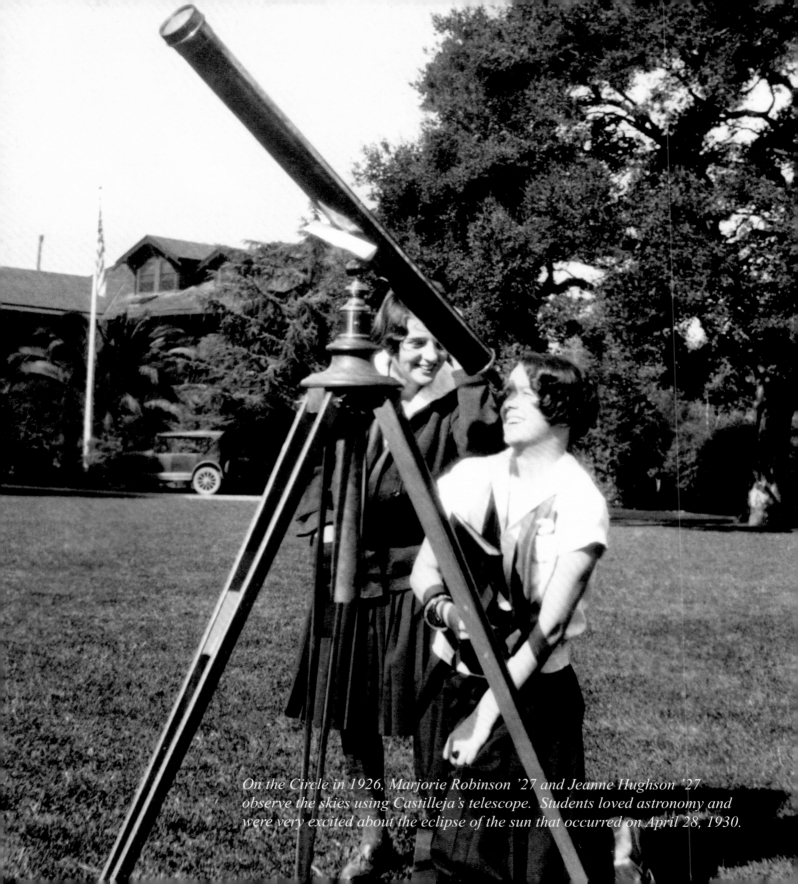

On the Circle in 1926, Marjorie Robinson '27 and Jeanne Hughson '27 observe the skies using Castilleja's telescope. Students loved astronomy and were very excited about the eclipse of the sun that occurred on April 28, 1930.

The Playhouse at Hidden Hollow

believing also that sound bodies aid in mental growth and in character development."[24] Miss Lockey believed that outdoor activity was essential because climate and setting influenced a child's education. Of course, Palo Alto's enviable environs were an impressive selling point. The girls played "tennis, volleyball, and basketball" competitively in "interclass and interscholastic" teams but also learned gymnastics, dancing, baseball, and swimming in their physical education classes, which aimed "to promote health and strength, and to develop ease and grace of body."[25] Today's athletic program and fitness and wellness classes have similar goals. Girls often assembled on the Circle to do their callisthenic "warm-up exercises." Horseback riding at neighboring stables was also popular.

Naturally, a woman who boasted that, weather permitting, physical education "is entirely out-of-doors"[26] would seek an even more natural environment for her pupils as the city of Palo Alto encroached on Castilleja's once sparsely populated neighborhood. In 1919, Castilleja purchased Hidden Hollow, a "permanent camp in the Santa Cruz Mountains."[27] Students could wade in La Honda Creek and sleep out in the open. An "artistic little cabin" with Japanese-style architecture known as the Playhouse completed this lovely get-away just fifty minutes from Palo Alto.[28] Today students retreat to the Santa Cruz Mountains, Pinnacles National Monument, and the American River for their outdoor adventures.

Having tended to their bodies and general health, Miss Lockey did not neglect the spiritual side of the students. Although the school was nonsectarian from its founding, her purpose was "to give definite training in ethics and religious principles, to deepen the pupils' regard and reverence for spiritual things, and to intensify their religious faith." While the school was not affiliated with a particular religious

The Sixth C: Construction

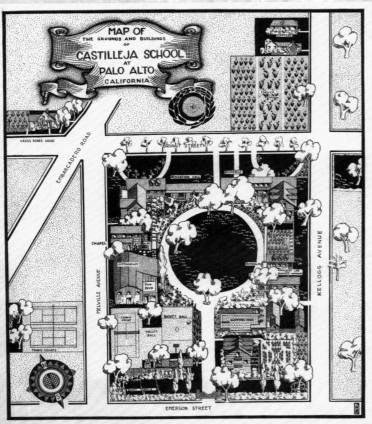

Ironically, considering the premium Castilleja puts on space today, the campus in the 1910s was sparse and underutilized. The new campus had only four buildings, no matter how hyperbolically Miss Lockey described them. By the time of her death in 1939, she had managed to optimize every inch of Castilleja's campus in a series of building programs. In 1921, the school built the swimming pool and Orchard House, which housed the music and art departments as well as the Infirmary. The class of 1913 presented the Rose Garden, and the next year's class gave the sundial at its center. The class of 1924 presented the grill used for many of the school's luncheons. Castilleja added a lab for chemistry and physics, a dramatic workshop, another cottage, a new primary wing, new tennis courts, and a gymnasium/auditorium as well as the Chapel. Built in 1926, the Elizabeth G. Hughes Chapel was the biggest undertaking the school had ever attempted, but (with remodeling in 2001-02) it still stands today, providing the venue for assemblies and performances.

Alumnae Corner
Achsa Barnwell '22

Achsa Barnwell learned to fly a plane after she graduated from Castilleja. She became a charter member of Ninety-Nines, an organization of women pilots founded in 1929. Amelia Earhart was a fellow member of the organization, named for the number of charter members. Ms. Barnwell titled her autobiography simply: Achsa. *She lived to be 100 years old. In an interview in 2002, she remembered her performance in the May Fete (see oval).*

denomination, students were almost exclusively Christian and predominantly Protestant. Residence students were expected to attend a church service each Sunday and bring a "reference Bible"[29] to school. If a girl's parents had not requested a specific church, she would attend services at the Stanford Memorial Church, where she would be given the "privilege of hearing excellent music and the best speakers from all over the world."[30] Additionally, a Sunday evening vespers service was held in the new Chapel on campus named for Elizabeth G. Hughes. The hour-long meeting was "devoted to a song service, to the study of the Bible, and to readings and special talks by the Principal."[31] Each day began with short "chapel exercises" that included hymns. The 500 seat Chapel was also used for "commencement exercises, recitals, and lectures."[32] While there is no question that speakers in the Chapel used religious language with a certain intent, the Chapel was never used as, or ever intended to be, a church. This focus on and implicit endorsement of religion, most specifically Protestant Christianity, was clearly stronger during this time than might be expected now for a non-sectarian school,

but the assumption of Christianity was neither unusual nor unwarranted for this era. During this period, there was little religious diversity in the area. According to *Palo Alto: A Centennial History,* the Palo Alto of the 1930s featured many Christian churches for various denominations as well as one Buddhist temple, but the city did not have a synagogue until 1954. Prior to that year, the nearest place of worship for people of the Jewish faith was Temple Beth Jacob in Menlo Park. Stanford was not much more diverse than its neighboring town for "only nonsectarian Protestant services were allowed at Stanford for many years; not until the 1960s did relaxed rules allow churches to have student centers on campus."[33]

Another facet of students' moral education came in their service to the greater community. In keeping with the ideals of her progressive education, Miss Lockey strongly encouraged service, feeling "training in social service" to be "of equal importance with that in any other field."[34] Students gave money to the Stanford Home for Convalescent Children, a United States Veterans' Hospital, the Lost Tribes of Indians in Datil, New Mexico, and "five French orphans whom

Top: Students during the 1931-32 school year do art projects about ancient Egypt.

Oval: Achsa Barnwell '22 plays Lightning in the May Fete dance program.

Top: In 1917 several students took a trip to Rigney Cottage in Carmel. Ruth Hartwell '17, Alicia Hill '18, Maria Hill '18, and an unidentified student enjoy a campfire.

Oval: Sybil Nowell '18 and Dorothy Jordan '17 carry a tickled Gertrude Emmons '16.

Below: This trophy for tennis doubles was first presented by Miss Lockey in 1923.

the school 'adopted' during the World War."[35] In addition, "the entire school took part in the Red Cross drive and filled about two hundred stockings for the annual Christmas Tree at the Stanford Clinics in San Francisco."[36] Miss Lockey was proud that "the girls themselves initiate and carry out plans for furthering their various forms of service" because she felt that "rendering genuine aid to less fortunate people is invaluable."[37]

Indeed, such an attitude is evident in several of the five Cs—overtly in charity, but implicitly in conscience and character.

The effort to build girls sound in mind, body, and soul was achieving outstanding results. Castilleja students were enjoying great success in college admissions. In 1935, the *Palo Alto Times* reported that 23 of the 27 Castilleja graduates were bound for college in the fall. Chosen destinations included Stanford, Sarah Lawrence, Bryn Mawr, Vassar, Mills, Pomona, University of Arizona, and Reed. Castilleja's 85 percent college

attendance rate is stunning, considering that less than 10 percent of women in 1940 who were 25 or older had spent any time in college, and only 13.3 percent of women whose high school graduation year was between 1931 and 1940 continued schooling after high school.[38]

Although nationally few women were pursuing higher education, this was an era when girls' schools were right in step with the times. Single-sex education was respected and even on the rise. Ilana DeBare, author of *Where Girls Come First*, notes that "the share of private secondary schools that were single-sex rose from 44 percent in 1899-1900 to 53 percent in 1919-1920—a sharp contrast from the nearly universal coeducation found in public schools."[39] Girls who went to single-sex schools during this era almost universally loved their experiences.[40]

It is thus no surprise that the early Castilleja alumnae were exceptionally devoted. Alumnae Day started during this period, but graduates often got together informally for tea.

These women certainly had plenty to talk about. Castilleja's early graduates were now out in the world. Margaret Willis '26 was the

THE HOOVER CONNECTION

Part of Castilleja's lore includes stories about a young Stanford student, Herbert Hoover, working as a janitor or general helper at the school. While this legend is not exactly true, Hoover did work at the earlier Castilleja Hall, and he maintained his ties with the later version of the school. In 1924, Mrs. Herbert Hoover spoke at Commencement, and Herbert Hoover Jr. married Margaret Watson '21. Miss Lockey became a delegate to President Hoover's White House Conference on Children. This conference produced the first Children's Charter, which named schooling, medical care, and a safe home as fundamental rights for all children. When Castilleja celebrated its twenty-fifth anniversary, President Hoover sent a warm congratulatory letter from the White House.

Top: Republican nominee Herbert Hoover, Mrs. Hoover with their sons Allan and Herbert Jr. as well as Herbert Jr.'s wife Margaret Watson Hoover '21

Below: Republican presidential nominee Herbert Hoover motors home on November 5, 1928—the day before the election.

Castilleja students were among the crowds welcoming the future President back to Palo Alto.

Top: Students use the chemistry lab during the 1926-27 school year.

Below: On the program for the Silver Anniversary Celebration, Miss Lockey's importance to the school is evident: the Castilleja C surrounds her portrait. The festivities included a birthday cake, the induction of the class of 1932 into the alumnae association, and a history of the school read by Miss Lockey.

"first woman to win an air pilot's license from the university branch of the Palo Alto School of Aviation."[41] Achsa Barnwell '22 was a charter member of the "Ninety-Nines," an organization of women pilots founded in 1929. Jeanette Maxfield Lewis '14 received the California Society of Etchers award for her drypoint piece, *The Beach,* at the M. H. de Young Memorial Museum in 1933.[42] Helen Sharp Thayer '16 taught medical microbiology at Stanford; Mabel Newcomer '09 was a professor of economics at Vassar College. However, many Castilleja graduates, like most women of their time, found prominence through their charitable work for organizations like the Junior League or their marriages to important men. Margaret Watson '21 married Herbert Hoover Jr., a Harvard professor and son of the future president of the United States. Some women had the best of both worlds. Mary Curry '12 married Donald Tressider, who became president of Stanford. More importantly, she also served as chair of the board for Yosemite Park and Curry County and later published a book, *Trees of Yosemite.*

Castilleja celebrated all its daughters,

seeing success in a woman's fulfillment of her hopes, whether those were private dreams or

Top: Helen Robinson and her class meet outside one day in the fall of 1923

Center: Castilleja kept tabs on their graduates by clipping out pertinent newspaper articles in the San Francisco Chronicle *or the* Palo Alto Times. *The school also kept any article that mentioned Castilleja itself. Dusty, crammed pages such as this one from August and September 1933 recorded marriages, divorces, travel, sorority pledges, and sports results. The local papers covered such breaking Castilleja news stories as the election of new class officers and the return of resident students from long holidays.*

public ambitions. Castilleja scrapbooks, which archived every newspaper mention of Castilleja

or its students, are as full of jubilant headlines about marriages and babies as they are of ones about public achievement. Alumnae news in the *Circle* also recorded the joy of more private accomplishments.

Castilleja had a lot to celebrate as 1932 saw Castilleja's silver anniversary. It was a simultaneous triumph for both the school and its founder because the two were virtually synonymous. Telegrams and letters poured in congratulating and thanking Mary Lockey. Beth Hughson, a Latin teacher who joined Castilleja in its second year, wrote thus: "I owe so much to Castilleja School, which means Miss Lockey! The tree inclines as the twig is bent, and never has a day passed but that I have been consciously appreciative of Miss Lockey's 'bending.' It was she who taught me that the future course of history depends upon the school of to-day… Under Miss Lockey, Castilleja School has given to the world the utmost of the worthwhile attributes of its students and faculty…We of Castilleja School are merely constellations that reflect the glory of the sun. Miss Lockey with her supreme charm and loveliness is our sun."[43]

President Herbert Hoover sent congratulations from the White House: "My dear Miss Lockey: I send you my cordial congratulations upon the completion of a quarter century of service in the cause of education which you have so helpfully forwarded, and my best wishes for many years more of success in

Top: Although the school did own an automobile called the "School Bus," students still often traveled in vehicles powered by other means, such as bikes and horse-drawn carriages.

Below: Telegrams sent to the school by Miss. Hughes, Helen Angier Bavington, and Johnnie (Joanna) Johnson Dubois to congratulate Miss Lockey on Castilleja's twenty-fifth anniversary

earning the affectionate appreciation of your pupils. Yours faithfully, Herbert Hoover."[44] *The Stanford Illustrated Review* featured its alumna: "Important and complex as Castilleja has grown to be, Mary Lockey is, as she always has been, its personification in the minds of those who know it best. What Castilleja is, she makes it. The high place it holds among the private schools of the country is a tribute to her ideals and her farseeing judgment."[45] The week of celebration included art exhibits, music and dance programs, and dinners and luncheons for alumnae, as well as the twenty-fifth commencement exercises. Indeed, Castilleja did have much to celebrate. In a quarter of a century, the school had graduated 634 girls, 166 of whom stayed in Palo Alto as Stanford students.[46]

Mary Lockey had grand plans for her school. At the celebratory dinner, Ena Douglass '30 announced the school's plan "to create a permanent foundation for the school, assuring its continuance as an enduring institution without the element of personal financial gain."[47] Miss Lockey bought back almost all of the school's stock in preparation for the organizational and financial restructuring of the school.

While Castilleja was celebrating, however, the country had entered grim times. Although Castilleja was untouched during the early days of the Great Depression, it too would begin to feel the economic hardships of the era. Grand plans for the future would have to be put on the back burner as Castilleja fought for its own survival.

Students enjoy a ride in a 1928 car.

825·560
19 CALIFORNIA 29

Zoe Kornberg '08 as the Candyland
lollipop princess at the banquet in 2006

JUNIOR-SENIOR BANQUET

"We take pleasure in presenting you with these rings, which formally bring you into the Senior Class. We hope you will always cherish them, and strive to live up to all that the C stands for."

—Margarita Espinosa

From the early years of Castilleja, junior-senior traditions have featured prominently in the calendar. The Junior-Senior Banquet celebrates the friendship and guidance of the seniors and the assumption of power by the juniors. The first *Paintbrush* in 1914 recorded, "It is a custom of the school for the Junior class to entertain the Seniors sometime near the close of each year. They have given hay-rides and picnics, and have taken the girls to moving-picture shows, but the class of 1915 proved its originality by inviting their departing sisters to a 'Thé Dansant' in the Residence." The event was often a picnic, but in 1926 the juniors threw a dinner for the seniors at the Oak Tree Inn instead. The change stuck, but it shifted from a country-club dinner to a themed banquet given in the Castilleja Residence. Preparations grew more elaborate with each year. By the 1940s, the banquet was a full-scale extravaganza with all the traditional songs, speeches, and ceremonies set against a painstakingly decorated theme background. Heaven, Shangri-La, Sidewalks of Paris, an Evening with the Gods, San Francisco, Twilight in Tahiti, Winnie-the-Pooh, Alice in Wonderland, Charlie and the Chocolate Factory, The Wizard of Oz, the Circus, and Pirates of the Caribbean are a few of the many themes that have been chosen over the years. Generally, themes are colorful, fun, and rooted in childhood memories because the banquet includes heavy doses of nostalgia.

Top: Sophomores B.J. Topol '86, Suzanna Gates '86, and Ann Brolly '86 in costume for the 1984 banquet

Center: The banquet in 1945

Bottom: Students admire their rings.

Inset left: Miss Lockey's invitation to the 1929 banquet

Inset right: Castilleja class ring from 1970

Below: Program for the 1932 banquet

STUDENT PERFORMANCES

"Castilleja has come into its own in drama. Perhaps the dramatic productions will soon achieve the acclaim that the musicals have enjoyed in the past."
—Elizabeth Schulte '83

Top right: Emily Glenn '99 leads the cast of the 1999 spring musical, Anything Goes.

Center right: Laura Scharff '10 gossips on the phone in Bye Bye Birdie, *the 2005 eighth grade musical.*

Bottom left: Castilleja students have always enjoyed performing Shakespeare. These tudents are in a 1923 production of As You Like It.

Bottom right: Eleanor Liu '04, Molly Fischer '05, Sara Croll '05, Iris Schimandle '05, and Chloe Leinwand '02 settle into their new secret home in The Diary of Anne Frank, *the 2001 fall play.*

Castilleja students have been putting on plays for almost 100 years. Oral expression was an early focus of Miss Lockey's curriculum, and students used their training to put on short plays in the Gymnasium Auditorium. Drama was also part of several academic courses, and in the 1920s the French Play and the English Play were regular highlights of the year. The Drama Club, sometimes called the Cats Paw Club, produced plays of all sorts. With the renovation of the Elizabeth G. Hughes Chapel to create a real theater in 1980, students had a state-of-the-art facility for performances, a venue that was improved further with the 2002 remodel. Some shows, such as *A Midsummer Night's Dream, Anything Goes,* and *The Diary of Anne Frank,* have proved to be perennial favorites. Performers and audience members alike anticipate the annual Upper School fall play, 8th grade original one-acts, Arts with a Heart, Middle School musical, and Upper School spring musical. In addition, student groups put on more informal productions, and drama classes teach every aspect of theater through original and classic scenes. Student theater brings culture to the school community and confidence to its participants. Castilleja students from every generation have enjoyed their moments on and behind the stage, and they continue to amaze, delight, and educate with every performance.

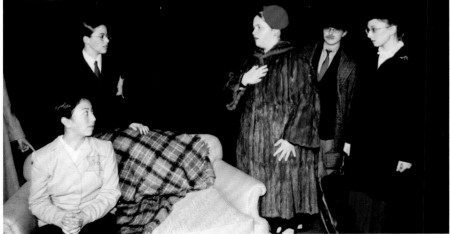

Chelsea Waite '07 and Sol Hilfinger-Pardo '07 in the 2006 production of A Midsummer Night's Dream. *The show was set in India.*

"Household Arts" was "designed to give the girls a practical and scientific knowledge of household economics." Classes for residents were required unless "preparation for College Entrance Board examinations makes it impossible" because the school saw a "great need in the American home for better training in the main business in life of the majority of girls and women, that is, homemaking." During the Depression, an era when many families had to stretch their pennies, knowing how to run an efficient home was a valuable skill.

Chapter Three
HARD TIMES

"The Depression was a real blow to [Mary Lockey] because everything had been going so well."[1]
—Margarita Espinosa

*L*ike most of America, Castilleja fell upon hard times in the 1930s. Not only was Miss Lockey in poor health by this time, but the nation was in the grips of the Great Depression. Although the school enjoyed general financial health through the 1920s, profits were put back into the school to continue the building program, so there was no reserve fund for emergencies. Castilleja, like all private schools, depended on the financial health of its families; those families struggled in the 1930s. Castilleja came very close to closing its doors because of debt and declining enrollment.

By the fall of 1930, it was clear that some parents were unable to pay the full tuition. The school's budget report noted that "last year so many patrons who had always paid promptly were caught by the crash after they had placed their children in Castilleja that we were left with accounts receivable amounting to more than $15,000.00 when school closed."[2] Registration

WISTERIA

The Lockey-era brochure, "Views of Castilleja School," devotes its first page to the campus's many "Gardens." In additon to the Rose Garden and the Flower Garden, the book noted the "Blue Garden, Roofed with Wisteria." Wisteria also grew on the overhangs of most of the buildings, such as the Primary Wing and the Residence. Today, wisteria can still be found growing on the Administration Building.

Top: Students playing basketball in the 1934-35 school year. Notice how the uniforms have changed in a decade.

Oval: Students dance during the 1933-34 school year. Although times were grim, students still found fun on campus.

"Both the school and the bank assumed that the school would soon regain students."

began to fall off quickly, and students continued to withdraw during each school year because of their parents' financial difficulties. The school survived the early years of the Depression by taking out a mortgage on the property for $75,000.00 from the American Trust Company in 1932. Both the school and the bank assumed that the school would soon regain students and that paying back the note would not be a significant problem. But registration continued to fall at a greater rate than anyone could have predicted. Miss Lockey budgeted for 41 residence students, but only 30 came, and only 119 out of the planned 125 day students matriculated in the 1932-33 school year.

Castilleja worked hard to increase enrollment and help families continue to send their children and pay their bills. For the 1932-33 year, the catalogue included a special insert noting a 10 percent decrease in tuition and music lessons, bringing down the cost for a day student in the upper school from $450 per year to $405. The school hired a firm to generate "leads" for new boarding students, primarily those whose parents were "all professional people with incomes more or less unaffected by stock market conditions."[3] But these efforts were not enough, and enrollment continued to decline. Although the school had hoped to at least hold ground the next year with 30 boarders and 120 day students,[4] by the time the 1933-34 budget was assembled, the school was planning for only 20 boarders and 80 day students.[5] Predicting enrollment remained difficult as Castilleja tried to budget appropriately and to attract students.

The school made every effort to decrease expenses. In 1933, staff salaries were cut by 21 percent, and payments were deferred from April 1 to July 15. Some teachers took five-year notes in lieu of the remainder of their contracted salaries. In her moves to economize, however, Miss Lockey was quick to point out that academic standards could never be compromised: "There will be more salary cuts, as there were before, and…every expenditure will be most carefully watched without, however, lowering academic standards."[6] Yet even with every conceivable economy, the school could not make ends meet.

Miss Lockey worked hard with the American Trust Company and with helpful parents and friends of the school to try to secure financing. They drew up plans to sell preferred stock, but it proved impossible to sell any kind of stock in the financial climate of the early 1930s. The school took out a large second mortgage, which allowed continued operation during the decade, but payments on this debt proved almost impossible when they became due because the financial situation had not improved significantly. Although the accountants remained optimistic, the financial situation was grim. Not counting depreciation, the school showed a net loss for 1931 of $4,420 and for 1932 of $17,716.[7]

As the school continued to search for funding, banks and potential investors needed justification for the survival of Castilleja. Advocates for the school pointed to past profitability, arguing that "it would appear reasonable to expect that when conditions again become normal, Castilleja School will receive its share of the expected increase in patronage."[8] While making these financial arguments, Castilleja's advocates also focused on the importance of Castilleja and its value for students and the community: "In a world where material values have failed to save man from suffering and loss, there is indeed a need for values that endure. Schools like Castilleja hold aloft the social and moral standards that the world must have to recover. The high standards of the school are reflected in the character and achievements of its graduates, who are 'carrying on' in these days of crisis, firmly supported by the training they received in their formative years at Castilleja."[9]

Although the school tried to keep its difficulties from the students, the upheaval of the Depression had an impact on them as well. Student turnover was high as family circumstances fluctuated. Castilleja helped struggling parents keep their daughters in school; it was willing to negotiate different payment schedules based on specific family circumstances, or in some cases take fine furniture in lieu of payment. With families moving in and out of the area constantly, student rosters were constantly in flux. Yearbooks of the period reveal that

Top: Nancy Burbank '40 learns about prehistoric times with her clay dinosaurs in 1936.

Oval: Barbara Snyder '42 and Margaret Hoover '42 read on the Circle.

In February 1936, students went on the annual Yosemite ski trip that was primarily for seniors.

many students left and reentered Castilleja in the early 1930s, and that the school graduated many seniors who spent only their senior year at the school. One class in the 1934-35 school year had nine returning and six new students in September, gained two more after "Christmas vacation," and lost another although she "returned, however, in time for Commencement."[10] Flexibility in enrollment became almost normal; continuity was made impossible by the financial climate of the day.

Although their school and probably their families were struggling, these spunky and spirited girls still had plenty of fun. One of the yearly highlights was the fall picnic at Hidden Hollow, where the girls were allowed to let down their hair a little. Each high school class picked costume themes such as "the rollicking, riotous crew of the Good Ship Castilleja"[11] or "heartless cannibals."[12] Students also participated avidly in sports, especially tennis, basketball, and swimming. The 1934 yearbook noted that a "baseball game between the boarders and the day-girls" caused the school gardeners to quake "with fear for their delicate flowers, which were greatly endangered by the home runs and stray fouls."[13]

Castilleja may have been struggling itself, but the school did not forget about those who were hurting even more. The proceeds from the Senior Fair, an annual carnival with themes such as "Mother Goose,"[14] "rustic" country fair,[15] and "Wonderland,"[16] were donated to the Stanford Convalescent Home. Having been "seized with the spirit of Christmas" in December 1934, the class of 1939 adopted a "poverty-stricken family," giving clothes, food, toys, and money.[17]

At this time, Castilleja started a new Christmas tradition. In 1932, the old Christmas

Top: The senior class costume theme for the fall 1938 picnic was WPA workers. Their choice indicates the students' awareness of the Depression and Roosevelt's attempts to curb it, such as the Works Progress Administration. The economic issues that were hurting the school were also affecting many of the girls' families.

Center: Castilleja's problems, with both finances and enrollment, are evident in the low number of applications for admission to Castilleja during this period. This application for the 1938-39 academic year is just a single sheet of paper. Parents were required to provide financial references as well as general references and to include the first payment of tuition, 50 dollars, with the application.

Top: Castilleja girls dance the "Red and White Waltz" in 1935.

Oval: Miss Lockey relaxes at the 1938 picnic. This is the last picture taken before her death and was used at her memorial service.

"*Each girl who has gone out from Castilleja has carried with her the results of Miss Lockey's teachings, fine principles, high ideals, and sound scholarship.*"

Jinks and other programs were abandoned in favor of a play relating the story of the jester and the Madonna that became known as the Christmas Pageant. Castilleja's treasured pageant remained an annual tradition for more than 50 years.

The Christmas Pageant was only one of the many opportunities for girls to perform. Students regularly put on plays in French and English and danced in the spring dance program. They worked hard practicing the varied numbers and often wore beautiful costumes specific to each scene. The program showcased "traditional folk dances," "modern" dances, and "novelty numbers" such as "Mop, Mop, Mopping" and "the Gingham Dog and Calico Cat."[18] In the classroom, on the playing fields, on the stage, and in their charity work, Castilleja students worked hard and tried to live up to the five Cs in an attempt to put some distance between themselves and the financial anxieties of the Great Depression.

In 1939, with the financial crisis still challenging the school, there came what could have been the final tragic blow. On March 4, 1939, after a short illness, Miss Lockey died. Her funeral service was held on March 7, Arbor Day, and was followed by a memorial in the Elizabeth Hughes Chapel. The student body, alumnae, friends, and family, mourned her loss and paid tribute to her memory by singing her favorite hymns and listening to an address by her friend Roy V. Reppy. In the April *Castilleja Circle*, the Alumnae Association described the memorial and appealed to alumnae to help the school in memory of Miss Lockey: "Her loss to the alumnae of the school which she created is irreparable. She was our leader and our loving and beloved friend, who kept her hold on each of us, no matter how many the miles and the years of separation that lay between. Each girl who has gone out from Castilleja has carried with her the results of Miss Lockey's teachings, fine principles, high ideals, and sound scholarship. And as her alumnae have scattered far and wide, they have extended her influence to the four quarters of the earth. Now it devolves upon us to see that this influence shall never die. She lighted the torch; we must carry it on. And how better could we do so—how better could we repay her for her life of devotion to us, and the rare privilege we enjoyed of having her as a teacher—than by

Top: The Chapel was set up for Miss Lockey's memorial service on March 7, 1939.

Oval: Miss Converse is all smiles at the 1939 picnic. She would quickly lose that smile when she realized the extent of Castilleja's financial problems.

Below: The Castilleja school mascot, the pony

bending every effort towards making sure that her school—our school—shall continue, and continue in the spirit in which she founded it?"[19]

Although she was getting older and had been experiencing declining health, Miss Lockey's death was unexpected. Plans needed to be made quickly to fill the position of Principal. Richard Lockey, Miss Lockey's brother, inherited Castilleja School on her death. While he was a strong supporter of the school, he was not involved in the management of the school except as an advisor. He soon appointed a temporary Committee of Managers to assist him with the administration of the school. In the same issue of the *Circle* announcing Miss Lockey's death, there was a short item titled "Administrative Plans" announcing that "Miss Miriam Sewall Converse will come to Castilleja on May first, 1939, as Principal. She was Assistant to Miss Lockey from 1928-1933, and has since been at Miss Spence's School in New York City. Miss Converse knows and loves Castilleja, and is well fitted to carry on the high ideals which Miss Lockey established."[20] Spanish teacher and alumna Margarita Espinosa was promoted to become Assistant Principal.

Few records from the year Miss Converse served as Principal survive, so very little is known about her short tenure. She suffered ill health and was unable to provide strong leadership for the school. In the January 1940 *Circle*, Miss Converse was referred to as a "guest," and the article noted that "we sincerely regret that her recent illness has prevented her taking an active part in the school life."[21] In a history of the school dictated by Miss Espinosa, Miss Converse's illness was stated more clearly; she "suffered a nervous breakdown in the autumn."[22]

By May, the Committee of Managers officially replaced Miss Converse with Sallie

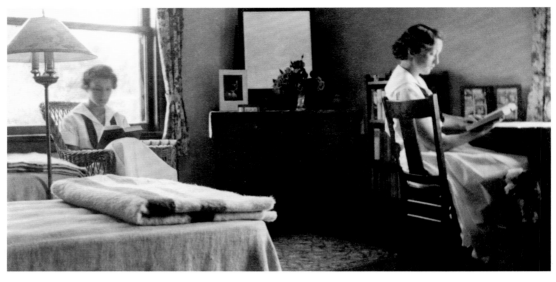

Top: Resident students Mary Sullivan '34 and Sally Merritt '34 study in their room.

Oval: Miss Wilson sits on the porch outside Recitation Hall examining the rosebushes growing around the building.

Below: Margarita Espinosa's 1940 Alumnae Luncheon invitation

Egerton Wilson, who arrived from "the cold of Washington D.C." into the "midst of a fully developed spring." She reflected on the warmth of the climate and then noted that "no less warm than the sunshine, was the welcome of Mr. and Mrs. Lockey, Miss Espinosa, the faculty, and the girls of Castilleja…It is a beautiful school, and I felt at home immediately." She went on to tell the alumnae "Of course I can never take the place of our beloved Miss Lockey with her inimitable personality, but I can try to carry on her ideas. I am happy to have known her, and, as I have long experienced in both eastern and western schools of the type of Castilleja, I hope I may carry on the traditions and high standards that Miss Lockey developed through so many years."[23]

Miss Wilson did not last long. Just as she must have done under Miss Converse, Miss Margarita Espinosa probably carried out the real work of the school in her job as Assistant Principal. Miss Wilson returned to the

East, because "apparently there were too many arduous responsibilities in this position for her,"[24] and in January 1941, Miss Espinosa became Principal of Castilleja School. In the class notes to alumnae, the change was announced with excitement: "Those of us who have known her as a teacher are certain of her ability, not only from an academic standpoint, but we recognize in her an executive with rare understanding. With poise and exceptional insight, she is able to grasp the problems of the girls or their parents, or faculty, and make the whole picture a harmonious one."[25] Although the school still faced almost unimaginable financial difficulties, the crisis of leadership was resolved. With the help of the Committee of Managers (who would soon become the Castilleja School Foundation Board), Miss Espinosa would guide the school out of the Depression and ensure it remained true to Miss Lockey's vision.

Students ride their bikes around the Circle in the fall of 1934.

Ericka von Kaeppler '09 plays waterpolo in 2005.

ATHLETICS

"We're dealing with the discipline and work ethics students get from their academics. Once they knew that what was expected from them in the classroom was expected of them on the playing field, the program took off."
—Jez McIntosh

Health and physical activity have been part of the Castilleja curriculum from the founding of the school. Miss Lockey, working with Miss Bolton of the Stanford physical education department, developed a program of outdoor physical education starting in 1907. Girls played tennis, Bostonball, volleyball, and centerball, but not basketball, because it was "too vigorous for girls." Ideas about girls' sports have changed since then, and since the advent of Title IX, girls have participated in college athletics in ever-increasing numbers. Participation in competitive sports became a cornerstone of the Castilleja experience. Olympians Nancy Ditz '72, Kate McCandless '88, Laurel Korholtz '88, and Amy Chow '96 may be unusual in their achievements, but not in their persistence and drive. Castilleja's athletics department currently offers 12 varsity sports in the Upper School and 8 sports in the Middle School. Upper School sports include basketball, cross-country, golf, gymnastics, soccer, softball, swimming, track and field, tennis, volleyball, lacrosse, and water polo. Middle School sports include basketball, soccer, softball, swimming, tennis, track, volleyball, and water polo. In 2006, over 70 percent of students participated in athletics. From 1998 to 2006, Castilleja has won 18 league championships and 17 league MVP Awards. Without a gym the 2006 Volleyball team made it to the division V state championship

Top: Dena Block '08 playing lacrosse in 2005

Center: Mika Peterman '05 playing basketball in 2005

Below left: soccer in 1998

Below center: Middle School softball in 2004

Below right: Tina Wray '89 plays tennis in 1987.

Inset: Middle School Athlete of the Year Award

FOUNDER'S DAY

"Sweet-scented memories return...
of a woman's quiet eyes and crown of silv'ry hair."
—"Our Day with Thee," Latham True

Top right: Jackie Provost reflects on her Castilleja experience in her speech at Founder's Day 1998.

Center right: Miss Lockey oversees the tree planting for Arbor Day 1919.

Bottom right: Members of the class of 2005 Sharlene Su, Nicole La Fetra, and Catherine Lee sing the Castilleja School song and are "proud thy crimson hue to wear."

Bottom center: Miss Espinosa leads the Founder's Day ceremony in 1941.

Bottom left: Laura Arrillaga '88, Pamela Hawley '87, and Karen Docter '84 plant the tree as part of Founder's Day in 1983.

From the earliest days of Castilleja, students and faculty celebrated Arbor Day by planting a tree or shrub and recounting the history of Luther Burbank and his creation of the holiday. Miss Lockey drew an analogy between the growth of a tree and the growth of a young girl. "Just as the tree develops a root-system in order to grow strong and beautiful, so does the young girl develop strong, healthy habits, and begins to build her own individual character. As she grows and learns from everything and everyone around her, her knowledge becomes the foundation for her role in life as a mature young woman." Miss Lockey's enthusiasm for Arbor Day made it an annual event. When the school moved to its current location, Miss Lockey lamented the barren campus, with "just twenty-two live oaks and nothing more" and used Arbor Day as an occasion to beautify the campus. In 1911, students planted an entire orchard. Mary Curry Tresidder '12 wrote the Castilleja Arbor Day song. In 1940, Arbor Day at Castilleja became Founder's Day, in honor of Miss Lockey and the holiday she loved. On Founder's Day, a senior gave a brief tribute to Miss Lockey and an overview of the history of the school. The biggest change to the tradition of Founder's Day came in 1965, when the event was combined with the Mother-Daughter Luncheon. By the mid-1980s, the tradition of having five senior speakers became central to the program. Miss Lockey would have loved to hear the reflections of these thoughtful, eloquent girls on their life at Castilleja and on the school's history. While Founder's Day has grown and changed over the years, remembering Miss Lockey's gift to us all is always the heart of the event.

Planting a tree on Founder's Day in 1961

The 1941 senior class displays a patriotic spirit as All-American Girls at the fall 1940 Hidden Hollow picnic.

Chapter Four
WEATHERING THE STORM

"It has for so many years contributed substantially to the preparatory work for girls in California that to close Castilleja... would be felt by many to be an educational and personal loss."[1]

Within the first two weeks of Miss Espinosa's appointment, Mr. and Mrs. Lockey and the Trustees announced to the new head of school what she may have suspected already but could not have known for sure: "The School was on the verge of bankruptcy and would have to be closed within a week as there were no cash funds to carry on."[2] But Miss Espinosa would not let that happen. She called an emergency meeting of the parents and kept the school open with a generous gift from alumna Pauline Chamberlain Fisher '20. The faculty agreed to go without pay, but the parents assessed themselves and insisted on paying a portion of the teachers' salaries. The financial state of the school was placed in the hands of a Management Committee. The school finished the year, but the future remained uncertain.

For many decades, Castilleja and Margarita Espinosa seemed to be one and the same. Generations of alumnae

STAINED GLASS

The window at the back of the Chapel was a "gift of the Alumnae Association, graduates, and former pupils from many parts of the world," in honor of Mary I. Lockey. Designed by artist Jeannette Dyer Spencer, the design consists of "three medallions, each symbolic of a phase of the education of girls." The window was presented at the 1941 graduation.

"It was not clear to anyone that the school would open in the fall."

remember her talks on etiquette, her stern discipline, and her dedication to the success of each Castilleja girl. But her connections to Castilleja had begun in the fourth grade. She was a member of the Castilleja class of 1922, although she had lived in Santa Barbara during her ninth grade year while her father worked for the military, decoding propaganda in South America, and she had transferred to the Convent of the Sacred Heart for her senior year. Born in Albuquerque, Territory of New Mexico, she had grown up in Palo Alto. Her father, Aurelio Espinosa, was a Stanford professor. David Starr Jordan had recruited him on the basis of his Ph.D. thesis "Folklore of the Southwest," which later became the definitive book on the subject. Miss Espinosa attended Stanford, where she earned a Bachelor's degree in Spanish in 1927 and a Master's degree in English in 1928 before returning to Castilleja first as a student teacher, then a Spanish teacher, and assistant to Miss Lockey. Her contract for the 1937-38 academic year specified a schedule of Spanish classes, regular parent and student conferences, and weekend chaperoning for a salary of $100 per month. She probably

never imagined then that Castilleja would be her home and her life's work for more than 30 years or that generations of Castilleja girls would never be able to imagine the school without her.

In the summer of 1942, Miss Espinosa was young and determined, but the financial situation was still dire. It was not clear to anyone that the school would open in the fall. The Management Committee negotiated with the Lockey family to create a non-profit organization to keep the school going in honor of Miss Lockey. With the help of one of the largest creditors, the American Trust Company, and Palo Alto lawyer Frank Crist, the committee negotiated with other creditors for patience.

Most of the creditors agreed to accept half payments, and the bank agreed to accept half interest. Local educators voiced support for the school. Aurelia Reinhardt of Mills College was effusive in her praise for Castilleja. "I hasten to assure you that Mills College is sincerely interested in the continuity of Castilleja and in the progressive success of its future work."[3]

In the fall of 1942, Mrs. Fisher, who had already shown her strong support of the school

with a substantial donation and her leadership as the head of the Management Committee, became the first Chair of the Board of Trustees for the new corporation. The other founding trustees were Frank Crist, Paul Holden, Nana Stevick Wells, and Marie de Forest Emery. Along with Miss Espinosa, the new Board would work tirelessly to put Castilleja back on its financial feet.

This fundamental change from private company to nonprofit organization was drastic but not unusual. Before the Depression had hurt the school so badly, Miss Lockey had already been working to convert the school into a nonprofit entity, in line with the trend in independent schooling. The National Association of Independent Schools had set up its membership rules to include only nonprofit institutions.

Over the next few years, several properties owned by the school were sold to pay back the debt. In the spring of 1942, the Management Committee sold the house at 339 Kellogg Street to John Kohler, who had rented from the school for the previous nine years. He paid $5500 cash for the property. The house at 343 Kellogg was likewise purchased by its tenant, Willard H. Sheldon, for $4500 cash. While later generations might regret the loss of these properties, there was no other way to keep the school from closing. Castilleja also found new ways to use the campus' outstanding facilities to both increase positive publicity and generate needed funds. In the summer of 1942, the swimming pool was open to the public from two to five every afternoon but Friday with an admission cost of 15 cents for children and 25 cents for adults. Swimming and diving lessons could be arranged for an additional fee. Alumnae were encouraged to come and bring their friends: "We want parents and children who do not know our school to become acquainted with it, and the swimming pool is a pleasant means of introduction."[4]

Castilleja also branched out with a summer program. Singing Trees had begun in the 1930s and continued to grow even through the financial troubles of the early 1940s. In the summer of 1943, the program expanded beyond the standard camp crafts, dancing, singing, swimming,

The Senior Fair for the 1939-40 school year had a Hollywood theme.

Top: Students jump rope in the spring of 1941.

Oval: V Is for Victory was the juniors' 1941 picnic theme. Students and teachers wore the button Peggy Slocumb '43 is wearing here, which shapes the Morse code V into the letter.

Below: A sign-up list for a 1943 Red Cross home-nursing class for students and teachers that met twice a week

and rhythms to include academic instruction in reading and dramatics. The school wanted to expand summer enrollment. To this end, the school offered a home economics course for ten high school girls in the Bungalow, giving high school credit and ensuring that the "social activities of this group of resident girls will be carefully developed and there will be maintained the Castilleja standard of living and chaperonage."[5] The traditions of summer camp have changed over the years, but today over 350 girls enjoy the campus every summer.

All these changes helped to temper the crisis. By February 1942, teachers' salaries were paid in full. But the enrollment problems continued. Miss Espinosa expressed her dilemma in a letter to current parents: "Our basic need is a larger enrollment. We have a beautifully equipped plant and a splendid faculty. All we need are students to avail themselves of this unusual opportunity for further development and thus acquire the poise and understanding so necessary in this war-torn, disillusioned world."[6] The dire situation could be seen in the numbers of graduating seniors: 33 in 1941, 20 in 1942, 14 in 1943, 15 in

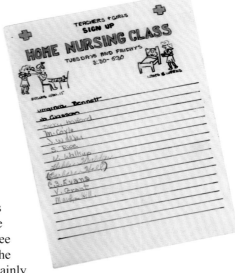

1944. The senior class of 1944 included only 5 returning students, and the combined freshman-sophomore class in 1942 was "surprised and pleased at having so large a class" of 15 students.[7] With the combination of the new management policies and the economic boost World War II provided, the situation would begin to improve. By the end of the decade, enrollment had returned to pre-war levels: the class of 1949 had 33 graduates.

The faculty, staff, and trustees did their best to protect the students from the financial crisis. The daily life of the school continued with minimal references to the desperate measures being considered in the Management Committee and Board meetings. The older students were certainly aware of the issues, and, in her June letter to the alumnae, Miss Espinosa congratulated the class of 1942 on their leadership. The seniors, she wrote, "have assumed the usual responsibilities of leadership in the school life—but this year they have done even more. Through a difficult time they have had a beautiful influence on the morale of the

Top: Students go out on the water at the 1946 picnic.

Center: Jo Glasson '43 drew an illustrated calendar for each week of the 1942-43 school year. Her cartoons illustrate weekly events as well as the war effort and the anxiety caused by exams.

"*Each member of the class made a 'sweater for British Relief' during their 'knitzkrieg'*"

school by their cooperation, resourcefulness, and selflessness." She thanked them for helping answer the phone, chaperoning younger students, and turning off unused lights, all without neglecting their academics.[8] The school found a way to turn its economies into virtues: "Difficulty in securing a domestic staff has resulted in simplifying the running of the residence in a manner comparable to the enforced simplicity of most present-day homes."[9]

As Castilleja struggled through its financial crisis, America struggled through a crisis of much more epic proportions. In contrast to the way the school tried to shield the students from fiscal problems, Miss Espinosa and the faculty made sure the girls were well aware of the rising global conflicts. World War II became an issue for most Americans in 1941. The students enthusiastically wove the war effort into the fabric of their lives. Even before the United States entered the war, the junior class theme for the Hidden Hollow picnic was V Is for Victory. Each member of the class made a "sweater for British Relief" during their "knitzkrieg," and the class achieved 100 percent participation in the Castilleja Red Cross Drive. After the "fateful Sunday which brought war to the United States," they all prepared for the annual Christmas pageant "in spite of blackouts and much war talk." The girls thought the Pageant "seemed much more

Top: Boys and girls in 1942 tend the school's victory garden.

Oval: Beverlee Parker '42 and Marirose Shenk '42 dress as members of the U.S. Army at the fall picnic in 1941.

Below: A 1942 poster reminds students to bring Christmas presents for soldiers and sailors.

Below: A 1943 Glasson cartoon

beautiful than ever this year. It left everyone with an appreciation of the true spirit of Christmas; also with the wish that the holidays could be more happy for the world."[10] The "Junior Class History" in the 1942 yearbook reveals the degree to which the war was present in their daily lives. Castilleja had a victory garden and encouraged students to buy stamps and war bonds.

The changes wrought by the war affected students' schedules and touched their psyches. The girls used creative outlets, such as the literature portion of the yearbook, to express their feelings. Many of their stories and poems reveal an understanding of the complex political and personal issues related to the war. Some express an admirable determination to "see this war through"[11] "until victory!"[12] while others focus on the gravity and horror, which "deprives children of their youth."[13]

Years later, Miss Espinosa reflected on the War years: "the blackouts in the Great Hall of the old residence, learning to wait on tables when our Stanford 'hashers' (many of whose daughters later came to Castilleja) left for battlefields in Europe or the South Pacific, picnics at the beach at twilight free of fear, the celebration in the Residence when trustees and students burned the mortgage–all stimulated a high degree of comradeship. Our gymnasium was designated as a center for refugees from San Francisco should the need arise. We were fully equipped and ready."[14]

But the war, thankfully, did not last forever. With the surrender of Japan, America breathed a sigh of relief. It was, if only briefly, the world's sole superpower, and its citizens were ready to relax and enjoy the luxury of peace. The tone at Castilleja was no different. The girls turned their energies to pursuits that were more frivolous but also more enjoyable after years of tension, deprivation, and sadness. While they still carried on in many of the activities and traditions from earlier years, their enthusiasm and energy were now devoted to dances and boys. Castilleja's student newspaper during this era, the *Laurel,* which started in December of 1945, devoted nearly half of its coverage to gossip, fashion,

and jokes. A fashion column titled "Bwang Bait" recorded in one issue that "Mary Jane wore a watermelon colored taffeta formal, featuring a drummed-up bustle effect in the back. It was very fetching…Oh! It almost skipped my mind: have you seen Nora's outfit? Why, not only is it out of this world, but it is the most devastating, and breathtaking color combination I've seen this year. Great heavens! As I look around me, I see that Maxie has copied her idea…why, so has Sue. Oh my! How rapidly fads spread!"[15] The column also advised girls not to copy the bobby-soxer fashion so "comfortable to the human body" yet so "annoying to the eye" that would make people "classify you as a 'bobby-sick, Sinatra fan'!"[16]

Although Castilleja girls of this time might seem rather preoccupied with amusements, they were still more academically oriented than most of their contemporaries. Nationally, only 15.7 percent of the women whose high school graduation year fell between 1941 and 1950 went on to college, compared with 24 percent of men the same age, a figure aided, no doubt, by 1944's GI Bill.[17] All but a few Castilleja graduates in this same period pursued further education;

every single member of the class of 1949 went on to college. In this era, Castilleja students, the majority of whom were blessed with both intelligence and socioeconomic privilege, attended Stanford, Smith, Mount Holyoke, Radcliffe, University of California at Berkeley, Mills, Scripps, Pomona, Vassar, Occidental, University of Southern California, and Wellesley, as well as various other state universities and junior colleges.

Clearly, the girls were squeezing in their academics, but this *Laurel* excerpt from the "Senior Class Activities" column makes their priorities clear: "Mattie has Bill under control. Dina has big plans for marvelous times with Jerry, a romance started by Cupid at the Valentine Dance…Marie Phillips, Cris Dove, Sallie Woodburn, Sylvia Bellis, and Pat Connelly spent an entertaining weekend here at Casti writing letters to their men—and incidentally—their term papers."[18] To be fair, marriage was a key priority in this era. The end of World War II saw a return of prewar gender roles, with an emphasis on marriage and family for women. The behavior of Castilleja girls, then, was completely appropriate for the era. By

Top: Fifth and sixth graders work on the study porch in the fall of 1942.

Oval: Jo Glasson '43 paints on the Circle. She illustrated school calendars with her charming artwork (also used in this chapter) during the war years.

Top: Students in the late 1940s socializing with boys at a school event

Center: The first edition of the Laurel, *December 1945*

The Laurel

"The last boys to attend Castilleja were members of the 1947-48 kindergarten class."

taking men seriously, Castilleja girls were taking their futures seriously. Boys as well as academics were an essential part of their preparation for life.

The students were not the only people at Castilleja looking to the future, a future that seemed increasingly secure. Enrollment, which had fallen to 91 students in 1942-43, was up to 235 students by the 1947-48 academic year.[19] Gaining admission to Castilleja was not especially difficult at this time, but the school did reach its capacity, having to declare some grades "closed" and turn a few prospective students away,[20] a welcome change from the desperate recruitment necessary in prior years. Indeed, with more girls than spaces, the school decided to cease enrolling boys in the primary grades. The last boys to attend Castilleja were members of the 1947-48

kindergarten class.[21] While it was sad to see them go, their departure was a testament to Castilleja's renewed security and prosperity.

The burgeoning enrollment was not the only way in which the school was expanding. the *Laurel* recorded the growth of the library with slavish devotion, listing all the new books acquired between printings of the biweekly issues, and Margarita Espinosa marveled in January 1947 that the library had 6600 books.[22] But one important item was shrinking: the school's debt. As of October 1, 1949, the school was officially out of debt for the first time since 1932.[23] This turnaround was nothing short of miraculous. Castilleja School, which had had no future whatsoever when Margarita Espinosa had taken the helm, had been saved from the jaws of death by its strong new Principal who would guide it through two more happy and prosperous decades.

Students at the 1945-46 freshman-sophomore dance

The Juggler, Pamela Wass '69, dances for the Madonna, Denise Hooper '69, in the 1968 pageant.

CHRISTMAS PAGEANT

"There is a tradition at Castilleja that is beloved and famous up and down the Peninsula, time-honored and hallowed. Everyone comes, not only alumnae, students, and their families, but people whose only ties with the school are their annual pilgrimage to Castilleja to enjoy the beauty and Christmas spirit of our pageant, The Juggler of Notre Dame.*"*
—The Laurel, *1948*

For 50 years, Castilleja students took part in this beautiful but, by the 1980s, controversial Castilleja tradition. Girls would wait their turn to try out for a lead, each hoping to be the year's Madonna, juggler, or prologue reader. The tale is loosely based on Anatole France's fable; each year, a new student-written prologue gave a slightly different telling—the lowly juggler gives the Madonna the best gift of all, her talent and her spirit, bringing the Madonna to life as the juggler is drained of hers. The production had no dialogue: the choir sang a wide variety of Christmas music, and the student monks chanted Psalm 148 in Latin. "The Jester's Christmas Story" was first enacted in 1932. By 1934, the pageant had been retitled, "The Juggler of Notre Dame," and had assumed the form it retained until its end. In the early years, the pageant was not held with absolute consistency, but the juggler's story struck a cord with many and was entrenched after the first decade. Sue Harris '57 wrote, "It is the juggler legend itself that is the fascination. It seems to get into one's blood and grow more lovely with time…At heart, I think we're all jugglers!" She loved the pageant so much she restaged it after Castilleja, once in a Muslim part of India and another time in England.

By the 1980s, the overly religious content of the program seemed inappropriate for a school whose religious diversity was increasing with each year. Today, Castilleja recognizes a wide variety of holidays under the direction of the Holiday Committee. While almost all agreed that the pageant was no longer fitting for Castilleja's community, many remember certain aspects of it with great fondness. An alumna from the early 1980s recalled, "This was one time of the year that every grade of the school got together for one purpose. It was crazy, with a special schedule for rehearsals, but it was everyone together for something important."

Top left: The choir sings during the 1969 pageant.

Center left: The monks in the 1948 pageant

Bottom left: Tanya Bauriedel '86, Nancy Allen '86, Jacqueline Taylor '87 and Elizabeth Cole '87 as the French nobility in the 1982 pageant

Left:Mary Severson '52 opens the 1950 pageant by reading the prologue written by Sally Kuechler '52.

FOOD

"While preferences for books or clothes change between grades, the love of Castilleja's food remains constant."
–Castilleja Paintbrush, *2006*

Top: Hope Fleming '41, Charlotte Goodwin '41, and Marion Marks '41 enjoy lunch outside.

Center: Sarah Shen '13 and Taylor Wilkerson '13 in the dining room in 2006

Bottom: Grammar school students drinking milk in the classroom

Right: These two cartoons from the weekly calendar were drawn by Jo Glasson '43.

Today, Castilleja's food service is a point of pride for the school. The school was "saluted" as one of three "shining examples" on the Peninsula where children and teenagers can "learn to love fresh, flavorful, and healthful meals" by Carolyn Jung of the *San Jose Mercury News*. Recent alumnae often lament the paltry offerings of their college meal plans when compared with years of fine dining at Castilleja. These same girls still think of Thursday as cookie day and remember that wallets left on the Circle were safe yet a cake might not be. As of the fall of 1998, food service is included in a student's tuition, a policy that facilitates lunch meetings with peers and faculty, but the program used to be optional. Beth Harris '77 remembers, "Most girls just brought their own lunches and sat out on the Circle." Castilleja's food service has not always been so universally beloved. Blair Stratford '56 recalls that "the food was good and the most famous was the cheese soufflé!" but Ellen Berger '59 remembers things slightly differently. Her description of meals served to Residence students includes such mouthwatering features as Thursday's " French Toast!! (two slices of white Wonder Bread; charred on the outside, squishy on the inside; bathed in slightly acrid 'maple' syrup)" and a lunch of "chipped beef in thin 'cream' sauce, smothering two slices of toasted white Wonder Bread, cole slaw (they didn't 'hold the mayo'!), and three cubes of pineapple (canned)." Students wore regular uniform for breakfast and lunch but were expected to dress up for dinner to varying degrees on different nights of the week. Special meals were the Tuesday-night grill, the post-church Sunday dinner of mutton or roast beef "with a strange 'rainbow' shimmer," and Sunday tea, a buffet of leftovers and fresh chocolate cake. Unlike other meals, it was served in "one of the Residence parlors" and boyfriends were invited. Georgie Gleim '69 recalls ever-proper Miss Espinosa "trying to chip away at" a frozen dessert that had come out too hard. From a 1930 sandwich sale raising money for charity to a bake sale raising money for the eighth grade Washington, D.C., trip, food has always been an integral part of the Castilleja student's life.

Antonio Valdivias and Rudy DeCaminada serving food from the grill in the kitchen

Students met "informally after dinner" in the "spacious living rooms" of the Residence according to the viewbook caption for this photo.

Chapter Five
RENEWING OUR PURPOSE

"Our eyes must always be turned alertly toward the future, without overlooking the cherished traditions and philosophy which have proved their worth over and over again."
—Margarita Espinosa

California, like the rest of the United States, in the 1950s and early 1960s experienced a growing population, an expanding youth culture, and the Cold War with the Soviet Union. The state's population grew by about 50 percent during the 1940s and by almost as much again during the 1950s.[1] When the baby boom generation began to enter high school, Castilleja had to expand. In an era of prosperity, Miss Espinosa and her staff could finally focus more on the institution and its students and less on the finances. As she looked forward to the fiftieth anniversary of the founding of the school, Miss Espinosa worked to improve and refine Castilleja's program, tweaking policies and embellishing traditions. Increased enrollment enabled the Board to make the pivotal decision to drop the lower grades, a choice that allowed an expansion of high school offerings and the hiring of many new teachers.

THE BELL

The Castilleja Bell was the gift of Louise Merrit Good '31. On the first day of school, the teachers who have been at Castilleja the longest ring this bell to signal the beginning and the end of the tie ceremony. Although a modern bell and intercom system exist for more practical purposes, the traditional sound of the bell on the Circle brings back memories for alumnae of many generations.

Top: Residence students enjoy their room on the senior corridor with its view of the foothills.

Oval: Miss Espinosa at the 1952 Christmas Ball

Below: Karen Garling Sickel '57 drew this cartoon of a Castilleja student using the phone.

Palo Alto, too, was growing, and Castilleja played an important role in the educational and social world of the mid-Peninsula.

Many of the traditions that began in the 1940s, or earlier, continued as the school thrived through the 1950s into the early 1960s. Although the nation was engaged in both the Cold War and the Korean War, the early 1940s taboo against amusement and entertainment during wartime relaxed, and students enjoyed a vibrant social life. Dances, from formals to mixers to barn dances, were held regularly and became anticipated highlights of student life, according to coverage in the student newspaper, the *Laurel*. The annual Senior Fair, which raised money for the Stanford Children's Convalescent Home, the Health Council, and the yearbook, became another popular tradition. For the fair, students decorated the gym with an elaborate grandeur similar to their preparations for the Junior-Senior Banquet. Like the banquet, the Senior Fair adopted a new theme every year, although the basic carnival elements remained annual features.

Girls engaged in a variety of student activities, from the rough-and-tumble of the outdoor picnics, games, and play days, when they competed against local schools in a variety of sports, to the more dignified traditions of the Christmas Pageant and Class Day. Blair Walker Stratford '56 remembers Class Day primarily as the day when the senior flag came down and the junior flag went up and, of course, when all the awards were given.[2] But before the transfer of flags, seniors bequeathed somewhat more imaginative items. Senior wills contained various bequests to juniors such as "my ability to write letters to boys," "my mother to any junior so that the junior may cut out for lunch," "my lady-like sneeze," "my job of opening the window in second period English class," and "my will power for dieting."[3] Sixteen-millimeter films shot of the Class Day ceremony show the great care and ceremony taken with both flags. The class flags were also important during Rivalry Week, when the juniors and the seniors

Members of the class of 1956 Vicky Bluford, Eleanor Williston, Sue Good, Blair Walker, and Bonnie Simrell enjoy the last days of May before their graduation.

Sylva McNamara '55, Guilia Tosi '55, Bonnie Muir '55, Suzanne Lake '55, Lucy Hume '56, Gari Wagner '55, and their classmates show off the Bungalow's cooking facilities.

Top: Students swim in the 1950 Aquacade.

Oval: Johnye Boyle '53 is having a blast at the 1952 Christmas Ball.

carried out all sorts of pranks, such as toilet-papering houses. Faculty houses were not spared. Like many alumnae, Stratford remembers that Rivalry Week, before the Junior-Senior Banquet, "was really a lot of fun." This spirit matched the lighthearted American culture of the 1950s. However, America's culture would soon move past this frivolous time, and Castilleja, like most schools of the period, would lag behind, holding on to ideas that became outdated.

In the 1950s, Castilleja maintained traditions, rules, uniforms, and other trappings of conformity. In addition to rules against tardiness, littering, rudeness, leaving campus, smoking, and cheating, students were warned against chewing gum, "wearing lipstick or colored nail polish while in uniform," "wearing any kind of clips or rollers in hair at school," and "eating anything or drinking Coke or any soft drinks in school buildings."[4] Committing two such offenses resulted in a "citizenship," the Castilleja equivalent of a demerit, and an additional 40 minutes in study hall. A student's name was read in Chapel and her punishment posted. "Talking during fire drills, whether going to the Circle or returning to class"

was an offense grave enough to automatically "warrant appearance before the court," in addition to an hour of Friday study hall.[5] A student from the class of 1956 recalled "The Latin teacher would stand outside the Chapel in the morning with a box of Kleenex, just in case anyone dare wear lipstick into the Chapel!"[6]

The rules were well-intentioned and helpful to some. An alumna from the class of 1957 reminisced, "During that time, our student days provided a ritualistic order which gave growing up a sense of predictability and a sort of—what I can only describe as—safety net amid the changes of adolescence."[7] But, however well this system had worked in previous years, the newer generation brought a different perspective on life and on authority.[8] Many students chafed at the rules, finding them silly, and, ultimately, some rebelled. Despite signing a "nonsmoking pledge" at the start of each year,[9] many students lit illicit cigarettes behind the tennis court or in Town and Country bathrooms. Residence girls tested their boundaries almost constantly. The *Laurel*'s January 19, 1954 column "Life in the Residence" reported that "Thursday night at exactly 10 p.m…the

"The Latin teacher would stand outside the Chapel in the morning with a box of Kleenex, just in case anyone dare wear lipstick into the Chapel!"

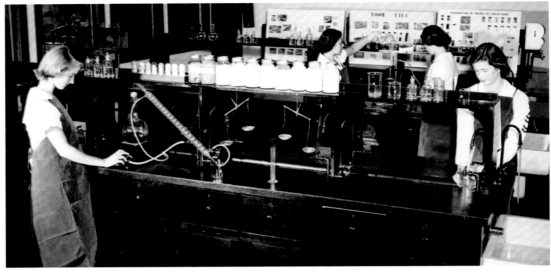

Top: Students work in the biology and chemistry Laboratories, where, according to the viewbook of the period, they gained "practical training in experimental methods."

Oval: A student and her date at the 1952 Christmas Ball

"Thursday night at exactly 10 pm...the junior hall was filled with sounds of shot-guns, backfires, and firecrackers."

junior hall was filled with sounds of shot-guns, backfires, and firecrackers (in reality, small paper bags exploded by the bomb experts in Casti's Residence). The juniors now have a new record, eight citizenships in fifteen minutes!"[10]

Students celebrated their own school spirit in the 1950s, even as they sometimes celebrated rule breaking. Barbara Finley '55 wrote an editorial in the *Laurel* the fall after her graduation to remind students of the importance of school spirit, which she defined not only as "going to games and yelling Rah" but also as getting good grades and observing the standards set by the student government. She warned, "If you want to continue to be proud of your school…don't disgrace it. If you lower the standards (and it's up to you), soon the fact that you go to Casti will mean nothing. COME ON KIDS, LET'S SHOW SOME SCHOOL SPIRIT THIS YEAR…DON'T WAIT UNTIL YOU GRADUATE TO APPRECIATE THE PRIVILEGE OF BEING A CASTI STUDENT."[11]

Alumnae of the era reflect on their years at Castilleja as ideal. Joan Knowles '52 remembers Castilleja's traditions and spirit, including Miss Espinosa's clapping her hands

to get their attention, the five Cs, and the way all of these things influenced her more as she grew older.[12] Residence students enjoyed trips to Stanford and San Francisco to watch plays and concerts and experience life outside the dormitories.

Although Miss Espinosa did strive to make her students aware of important issues both modern and global, the school did not leap to embrace America's budding social conflicts.

The Castilleja girls of the 1950s and early 1960s, like many of their Palo Alto peers, were geographically isolated from the civil rights battles of the era, but they could not remain ignorant of the issues. At this time, Castilleja did not have any African American students, and, on the basis of the demographics of the area, most girls were unlikely to be part of diverse social groups. The girls, steeped in the message of the five Cs, still proved surprisingly enlightened for their era and social background. Some girls did show an ignorance and insensitivity that is highly regrettable but not uncommon for the period, such as staging Senior Fair entertainments in blackface, but others displayed a heartening perceptiveness and sense of social

justice. In a short story published in the 1957 *Paintbrush,* Linda Tharpe '58 wrote about a group of college girls on a train who defended an African American classmate's right to sit in the same car with them. An alumna from the class of 1956 teaching at the Manual Arts School in Los Angeles wrote to the school community in the spring 1964 *Castilleja Circle* about her experiences. She urged her readers to get past stereotypes and meet people of different backgrounds.[13]

These varying attitudes show that Castilleja students were thoughtful and well-intentioned, demonstrating the conscience and character the school aimed to instill. These attributes were on display in more-pedestrian aspects of life as well. The role of student government expanded significantly with the creation of an honor code in 1953. With the honor code came increased student privileges, such as student-proctored study halls.[14] The students regulated themselves, with supervision from the administration, through the student court, the equivalent of today's Judicial Committee. Miss Espinosa praised the student court for their "constructive and commendable" activity and reminded parents of the important job the court had and of the "tremendous growth" seen in a "more mature attitude, and a gratifying sense of responsibility." In the same letter, she lamented that "there are some parents who do not seem to wish their daughters to accept responsibility for their conduct."[15]

Students were not the only ones taking on greater responsibility and involvement. In the 1950s, parents became more involved in the life of the school. The Mothers' Club started. Fathers and daughters began to enjoy the annual Father-Daughter Barbecue, a tradition that evolved into the Father-Daughter Dinner Dance by the late 1980s. Although Miss Espinosa praised the Mothers' Club, she thought parents should not be so opinionated about school matters and should

leave important decisions to the staff. Still, she certainly appreciated their help with fundraising. She wrote to the alumnae of the creation of the Mothers' Club in May of 1953: "Each year seems to bring something new to Castilleja. This year has brought to us an active and interested Mothers' Club ably led by Mrs. Fred A. Titus, mother of Jean Titus...Their interest in the school is most gratifying, and everyone is helping with their first project, heating equipment for our swimming pool, which will, we hope, greatly lengthen our swimming season."[16] Regular reminders to mothers about lost-and-found items and the importance of attendance show clearly how Miss Espinosa would have liked the mothers to spend their energy. "It will be appreciated if mothers will look through the collection of unclaimed sweaters, scarves, shoes, coats, etc., now in Miss Huckvale's office before the Christmas holidays."[17]

The Alumnae Association, too, was getting increasingly active. Miss Espinosa reported school activities to alumnae twice every year in the *Castilleja Circle* and always encouraged alumnae to visit frequently and keep in touch. In June of 1950, at the alumnae reunion luncheon, a tradition began when three staff members, Helen Snyder, Eleanor Huckvale, and Muriel Millington, were named honorary members of the Castilleja Alumnae Association and received Castilleja pins for their more-than-20 years of service. This tradition continues, although faculty and staff now become honorary alumnae at the alumnae induction lunch at the conclusion of 10 years of service.[18] By the late 1950s, the Alumnae Association, in addition to hosting the traditional June Alumnae Luncheon at Castilleja, held special area luncheons in San Francisco, San Jose, the East Bay, Menlo Park, and Portland, Oregon. One of the most important projects of the Alumnae Association was to raise money for the Mary I. Lockey Scholarship Fund.

The first Dessert Bridge Fashion Show was held on Valentine's Day, 1950; the theme was Hearts and Flowers. The event was deemed an "overwhelming success" and, because of the "most gratifying" response, became an annual tradition,[19] although it changed over time. In 1954, the "Alumnae Board voted to have a Spring Garden Preview and Tea instead of a Fashion Show."[20] Over the years, this event, together with the Senior Fair and the Mothers' Club's Holiday Table Setting Tea started in 1954,[21] evolved into many different fundraising events, such as the Tablesetting, the Senior Event, and the Benefit.

Seeing Castilleja alumnae reinforced Miss Espinosa's commitment to maintain Miss Lockey's mission to prepare young women for university and for life. The viewbooks of the early 1950s describe the purpose of the school this way: "Bearing in mind the need of girls for an adequate foundation to meet the special problems which womanhood faces, and of youth in general, to meet the demands of the complex life of today, Castilleja seeks to develop the innate capacity of the individual child, encouraging the pupils in independent and constructive thinking."[22]

And even in an era when the majority of young women did not see education as a career step, Miss Espinosa upheld Miss Lockey's priority: a rigorous academic program for high school girls.

Students recognized the importance of the Castilleja faculty and staff. They dedicated several yearbooks to beloved teachers and staff: Miss Huckvale, the Administrative Assistant; Miss Grant, who taught science and math; Miss Martin, who taught history; and Mrs. Twiss, who taught Spanish. Blair Walker Stratford '56 remembered her friendships with her teachers as one of the best things about Castilleja.[23] The faculty provided academic excellence, controls on behavior, and models of adulthood for students. When Miss Cooke was married in 1954 and changed her name to Mrs. John Reed Irwin, the *Paintbrush* staff dedicated the yearbook to her but insisted they would always remember her as "our Miss Cooke," because her spirit had "left a permanent impression in our memory."[24]

Educational historians have characterized the 1950s as a period when private schools often calcified or fell back on such conservative traditions that they lost the spark

"Each year seems to bring something new to Castilleja."

Kindergarteners enjoy their playground during the 1950-51 school year.

Top: Students pledge their allegiance in Chapel, led by Virginia Valentine.

Oval: Miss Espinosa addressed the student body in the chapel every Monday on topics such as manners and morals.

of innovation and creativity so important to their founding. This trend, while present, is less evident at Castilleja. Miss Espinosa might have been a stickler for appropriate behavior, but she did not want her girls to neglect global issues just because World War II had come to a successful close. Miss Espinosa exposed her students to the ideas, people, issues, events, and controversies of the day. In 1950, students listened to Allen Nicholas talk about the United Nations during U.N. week; in 1956, the *Laurel* highlighted the importance of the polio vaccine; and, in 1958, Princess Catherine Caradja of Romania brought her story of living "behind the Iron Curtain" to a special assembly. Miss Espinosa supported these aspects of the curriculum, but their inclusion meant that she sometimes had to protect her faculty from the political excesses of the Cold War era. When a student reported to her parents that Dorothy Feldmann's comparative government class included a unit on Communism, they called the F.B.I. But when an agent brought the matter to Miss Espinosa, she responded with a chilling look and said, "Communism? At Castilleja?" She sent him away, and nothing more came of the issue.[25]

By 1960, the topics of world affairs had become integral to the curriculum, and the new economics teacher, Peggy Algeo (now Mrs. McKee), was praised for bringing guest speakers to her economics and American government classes. In addition to a guest from the Stanford Business School who spoke about the history of the stock market and a professor from Berkeley who talked to the girls about money, Miss Algeo brought Lt. Norman Sylvester to speak "on the subject of limited war and the continuing importance of the infantryman in this nuclear age." Having served in the Marine Corps at Guantánamo Bay, he also spoke about Castro and U.S. relations with Cuba.[26] Sue Harris-Wilson '57 recalled that Miss Espinosa had "opened my eyes to the world beyond California" by encouraging students to learn about the world; Harris-Wilson went on to teach in England and Pakistan, as well as in the United States.[27] In keeping with the educational trends of the era, Miss Espinosa told alumnae that in the 1958-59 school year there would be "adjustments in the mathematics and science courses to keep abreast of new developments in both fields."[28] Castilleja would not be left behind as the country

"When a student reported to her parents that Dorothy Feldmann's comparative government class included a unit on Communism, they called the F.B.I."

Top: Students working in proctored study hall during the 1962-63 school year

Oval: Grace Wing '57 plays Hetty in Overtones, *one of the three plays presented by the Drama Club on March 17, 1956.*

challenged the Soviets in space and in the Cold War.

Castilleja fulfilled a range of academic needs and aspirations, from those of the highly intellectual students to those of some new students who needed "work in remedial reading."[29] It aimed to prepare all the girls, whatever their starting point, with the necessary training for college. In a letter to parents, Miss Espinosa clarified the school's mission: "As word has come to us that some parents do not have a clear idea about some phases of our college preparatory programs, I wish to take this opportunity to explain that Castilleja is primarily college preparatory. Ninety-nine percent of each graduating class enters colleges east and west, and Castilleja is fully accredited….A certain percentage of each graduating class cannot qualify for entrance to major colleges for various reasons, but we make every effort to place our graduates in the colleges best fitted to their needs, interests, and abilities."[30] Even at a time when most girls were being educated with the idea that they would be wives and mothers, rather than working women, Castilleja saw the inherent value of

raising educated and aware young women who understood that learning "is an active process" of using "all the facts and information you have acquired, correctly and effectively, and fit[ting] them together," not "merely read[ing] a certain number of pages."[31]

Miss Espinosa was proud of Castilleja's goals and wanted to publicize the school's mission. In the early 1950s, when she still felt the need to attend to enrollment figures, Miss Espinosa frequently appealed to alumnae for their help in this endeavor. "Won't you tell your friends, in fact, everyone you know, about our program, our academic standing, and our broad variety of activities, designed to take care of every phase of a girl's development? Also, if you have the opportunity, having enjoyed the advantages of independent education, will you…make a point of informing others of the unique benefits of independent education and its importance in the maintenance of the democratic way of life?"[32] Her concerns seem unfounded, since the following December she informed alumnae that Castilleja opened in the fall "with a good enrollment" and the school was "obliged regretfully to turn away many

fine girls…" in several grades. However, the need for Miss Espinosa and the Board to defend the value of independent schools in modern America persisted as an important element in school publicity through the 1950s and 1960s, especially during large-scale building campaigns. The students, too, pointed out the advantages of their school in the *Laurel,* and they cited the same thoughts as adults about private schools: smaller classes, wide selection of courses, cultural and social training, and superior preparation for college. The girls, however, did complain that "boys are the only things we lack," a lament that probably did not bother their parents. [33]

With such successes and such a solid sense of purpose, Castilleja had reason to celebrate its golden anniversary in 1957. The senior class dedicated the *Paintbrush* to "our beloved Castilleja…we offer our deep appreciation and gratitude, not only for the knowledge gained through the pages of books but for the knowledge of life and realization for success in our journey we must ever strive to achieve in our womanhood: Courage, Conscience, Character, Courtesy and Charity."[34] The theme of the yearbook was Then and Now,

and the book included photos from the early years of the school with current students striking identical poses. The Senior Fair, with a theme of "Fifty Years in Review," included entertainment numbers from 1907, 1927, and 1957. Miss Espinosa wrote to alumnae, "I hope that during this year more of you than ever before will visit your school and renew old ties. It is pleasant to reminisce, and it is gratifying to look back over what has been accomplished and to look ahead toward a promising future. This year we have the largest enrollment in the history of the school, and have had to turn away desirable applicants in both resident and day departments. With our new Latin room adjoining the history room above the chemistry laboratory and a longer school day, we are able to accommodate a large enrollment, but a pressing need, if we are to continue it, is more library and study hall space."[35] This anniversary, like the Centennial today, was a time to celebrate the past, but it was also an opportunity to look to

Sarita Coffin '60 and Barbara Leep '61 welcome French president Charles de Gaulle to Palo Alto on April 28, 1960.

the future and evaluate Castilleja's program.

It was the continuing success in enrollment in the Upper School that led to the decision to drop grades one through four in the fall of 1958. Miss Espinosa and the Board decided to improve the college preparatory program by paring down their offerings and becoming primarily a "secondary school."[36] It must have come as a surprise to many parents when they received a letter at the end of March 1958 informing them of a change in "policy which will affect your daughter's enrollment at Castilleja for the coming year." This was a euphemistic way of saying that their daughters could not attend Castilleja in the fall. Miss Espinosa did recognize that this notice was a bit late, noting that "we are sorry that this decision could not have been reached sooner, and hope it will not cause you undue inconvenience." Ever optimistic, she closed with the "hope" that "you will consider Castilleja again when your daughter is ready for the fifth grade."[37]

Miss Espinosa and the Board made this difficult decision for several reasons. They wished Castilleja to maintain its "outstanding" college preparatory record and felt that the lower grades hurt the school's ability to sustain and improve that record because the school could not specialize adequately. [38] The space devoted to the lower school was needed for other purposes, such as "study halls, library facilities and playgrounds, as well as classrooms." Castilleja's campus, at "approximately 5 acres," was considered half the "desirable area for 300 students."[39] Grades one through six were also operating at a financial loss, with costs per pupil exceeding tuition. Worst of all, the school realized that the lower grades were not feeding into the upper grades. In the five years preceding the decision, 76 percent of graduating seniors had attended Castilleja for four years or fewer, and 89 percent for six or fewer.[40] With the decision made, Castilleja moved forward with its plans for improvement. Although Miss Espinosa noted that "we miss grades I to IV in their little gingham jumpers," she, and the rest of the school, knew that the addition of a "beautiful and practical new Library and Study

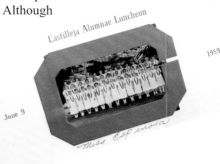

Top: Students sing during the 1962 dedication ceremony for the new residence.

Oval: Dusty Rhoades speaking at the groundbreaking ceremony for the new residence in 1961

"*Castilleja embarked on an ambitious building plan encompassing nothing less than the replacement of every building on campus.*"

Hall in place of the old primary wing" was more important.[41] By the fall of 1962, Castilleja, which only a decade earlier had been a K-12 school, finished its desired transition into a "six-year secondary school," comprising grades 7-12, and thus following the "accepted 'junior high' school" and high school models.[42]

Having made the decision to focus on a more limited age group with a more defined sense of purpose, Castilleja embarked on an ambitious building plan encompassing nothing less than the replacement of every building on campus. The March 1960 *Castilleja Newsletter* was a special edition dedicated to the development plan for the future. It noted that Castilleja's "buildings are time-worn and inadequate for a modern-day school with an enrollment of 260 girls."[43] The construction of a new Residence Hall was the "logical first step" in the plan to update all the facilities on campus. The structure we know today as the Arrillaga Family Campus Center was formally dedicated on May 24, 1962.[44] It could house 90 students in double rooms with a television lounge on each floor and a "large rumpus room" where students could "enjoy Ping-Pong,

records and Cokes."[45] The next project would be Rhoades Hall, a building with 20 classrooms to accommodate the maximum projected enrollment of 300 students.

Although the original plan that called for replacing all of the campus buildings was never completed, the building campaign marks the shift from an intimate and informal learning community to a more sophisticated institution. But in failing to complete the ambitious plan, the school preserved the beautiful architecture of the Chapel and the Administration Building.

The building campaign is symbolic of Miss Espinosa's greater challenge. She struggled to keep Castilleja's best traditions while still providing a modern, comprehensive, and socially responsible education that prepared young women for life in an ever-changing world.

A glimpse of the campus after the construction of the new dorm but before the construction of Rhoades Hall

Students, like these seniors from the class of 1997, look forward to getting their yearbooks at the end of Class Day every year.

STUDENT PUBLICATIONS

"We make no attempt to issue a pretentious school paper, but one that will fully chronicle those events of a busy school year, which are worthy of note."
—*1914* Indian Paintbrush

Castilleja's first student publication, *Indian Paintbrush,* appeared in 1914. It was a yearbook, with student photos and a review of the important events of the year, but it was also a literary magazine, with stories and poems, and an alumnae newspaper, with notes from the classes and news about the goings-on at school. As printing technology became cheaper, student publications grew and multiplied. *Paintbrush* became longer and included more photographs. In the 1940s, the Lower School began its own literary magazine, the *Flame*. In the early 1950s, *Paintbrush* changed in format to include photographs on every page, and the students created a new literary magazine for the Upper School, *Mochuelo*. The first school-wide student newspaper, the *Laurel*, began publication in 1945. The first editor-in-chief, Mary Iskason '47, wrote, "We shall try to present all the school activities in an unbiased, true journalistic manner." With that standard, Castilleja students continue to publish. In 1974, the name changed from *Laurel* to *Counterpoint*, and in the 1990s, the publication split into two: one weekly, one monthly. In 1999, students founded a second paper, the *Castilleja Free Press*, devoted to politics, world issues, and school news.

Top left: Counterpoint Weekly *is delivered to student mailboxes.*

Center left: Yearbook photographer Ali Aronstam '09 in the fall of 2006

Inset: The 1999 Mochuelo

Below left: Katherin Li '03 edits Counterpoint *in 2002.*

Below right: Caddie Heddleson '04 reads Counterpoint Weekly.

DORM

"Ask any dormie... living in the dorm is like a year-long slumber party with homework."
—1994 *Paintbrush*

Top right: Dorm living meant doing your own laundry.

Center right: A student relaxing in her room in 1985

Bottom left: Decorations made dorm rooms feel more like home.

Bottom right: Courtney Rowe '88 and another student talk on the phones in the residence.

When Miss Lockey established Castilleja, she recruited residence students, as well as day students, for all the older grades, designing a boarding program that emphasized health, fitness, and family-style living. The students came from all the western states and territories as either full-time or five-day boarders. In 1921, Miss Lockey published a guide "To the Resident Girls of Castilleja School" which set out the rules in eight pages. The introduction pointed out to the girls that, "Your happiness, so far as it is possible, is of the greatest concern to those of us in charge and it is with this in view, together with a desire to help in the development of fine and charming womanhood, that these regulations have been formulated." Not all boarding students remember the rules fondly, but most would agree that the residence was a place where they found friends and happiness. Sharon Gerbode '97 remembered moving into the residence in the middle of the year and finding that she "had twenty-eight new sisters and a crazy, lovable dorm-mother named Janet who would always be there for me." After a peak enrollment of 80 students in the 1960s, the numbers declined until the Residence Program closed in the 1990s. The school gained a language wing and a balanced budget but lost valued diversity from the many international students, especially those from Hong Kong, who had made the residence their home.

Residence students enjoy music and magazines in the 1960s. The record is Jazz Impressions of the USA *by the Dave Brubeck Quartet.*

Carol MacKenzie '68, Kathryn Klobertanz '68, Hilary Harts '68 and their friends watch TV in the senior dorm.

Chapter Six
INVESTING IN THE FUTURE

"You can leave your money to that big school just up the road, and nobody will ever know about it....But if you give your money to Castilleja, someday you will drive around the corner from Embarcadero...and say with pride,'That's my little old school.'"
—Dusty Rhoades, Chairman of the Board of Trustees

Cynthia Swanson Miller '64 was right when she reflected on her senior year: the death of President Kennedy sent a shock wave that penetrated to the very heart of Castilleja and marked a shift of perspective as students began to look "beyond our cocoon here at Castilleja."[1] Miss Espinosa always tried to impart an awareness of significant global issues to her girls. In the latter half of the 1960s, Castilleja girls internalized the message and began to seek out and investigate controversial ideas themselves. Students all over America were talking about serious issues, and Castilleja students were no exception. In the spring of 1965, Castilleja formed a chapter of Junior Statesmen of America.[2] The *Laurel*'s coverage of their first convention noted the "sophistication

CASTILLEJA TIES

Long colored ties have been part of the Castilleja uniform for almost all of its history. The current colors and traditions became a staple with dress whites in the 1970s, but earlier versions were all black, all red, or other combinations of colors. The tie colors stand out on dress white uniforms: yellow for sixth grade, light blue for seventh, navy for eighth, green for ninth, orange for tenth, purple for eleventh, and red for twelfth.

demonstrated among its members," who "were familiar with current events, current laws, and problems which we face today."[3] The topics discussed included "legalizing the dispensation of marijuana," "lowering the voting age in California," and establishing "less stringent laws on abortion."[4] Throughout the decade, the student paper covered difficult topics such as the Vietnam War. In February 1965 the *Laurel* argued that the "United States is simply not geared militarily or otherwise to deal with the Viet Cong and win the war."[5] It called the Ku Klux Klan an "evil menace to our country,"[6] and it called for sex education in schools.[7]

Encouraged by the enthusiasm displayed by Castilleja's budding politicians and journalists, Miss Espinosa continued to broaden the school's coverage of current events and issues. In a 1970 letter in the alumnae magazine, Miss Espinosa noted "Last year at Castilleja, students experienced a number of 'firsts' in the school's history. On November 14, the day before the national moratorium on the Vietnam War, the entire student body held an inquiry day into the issues of the war. Requested and arranged by the students themselves, the program presented different possible stands on the war, the panel being moderated by a professor of political science at Stanford University. On an earlier day, Professor David Kennedy, a Stanford historian, had [addressed] the student body [on] the history that lies behind the Vietnam conflict."[8] But Castilleja was not merely focused on the watershed issue of the day. The same letter notes that another spring highlight was "Anti-Doomsday," a full-scale conference held on April 21 on problems facing the environment. A lecture by D. Douglas Daetz, assistant to Stanford professor Paul Ehrlich, well-known author of *The Population Bomb,* first sparked interest. Then, on the day of the conference, professors, politicians, authors, and concerned citizens presented ideas in nine different workshops. The topics included "Do Cars Have a Future?," "South San Francisco Bay—Airport or Wildlife Refuge?," and "Should We Ban DDT?"[9] Castilleja reflected the cutting edge of the renewed environmental movement. The first Earth Day took place in

Miss Espanosa speaking to the school in chapel

Students singing at the dedication of the new residence in 1962

April of 1970. Students from the 1970s often recall that the environment, water conservation, and recycling were important topics for them throughout the decade.

Castilleja was not just talking about change; the school was living it. "The late '60s and early '70s brought one particularly historic change to the small world of elite girls' schools—integration."[10] Castilleja was at the vanguard of this development, enrolling its first African-American student, Colett White, as a freshman in the fall of 1965. Although she left Castilleja after her first year, Judy Lawrence joined the same class as a junior in the fall of 1967 and in 1969 was the first African American graduate of Castilleja. On her yearbook page, she quoted from George Bernard Shaw: "Some men see things as they are and say why: I dream things that never were and say why not."[11] She lived her ideal and threw herself into life at Castilleja. She was on the *Paintbrush* staff, in the drama club, in JSA, on the Social Committee, on the House Council, on the Student Council, and on the basketball and volleyball teams. Miss Espinosa was proud that the school was able to reach out to a diverse population,

but she lamented the lack of a well-funded scholarship program that would allow Castilleja to admit those who were "scholastically rich but financially wanting." At this time, Castilleja, like much of white America, associated racial difference with lower socioeconomic status, and Miss Espinosa was able, in the mid-1960s, to find individual area families to sponsor financially needy African American students.[12] In addition, Castilleja had long had a smattering of international students and boarding students from Central America, South America, and Europe and had more recently started accepting students from Asia, especially Hong Kong.

Although the school's intent was noble, the language used and attitudes expressed about issues of diversity sound old-fashioned and almost offensive to today's ear. Even Castilleja's 1978-79 WASC self-study described the school's "diverse" population in terms of socioeconomic status and race: "The majority of students come from middle- or upper-class families. However, the scholarship program (about 25 percent of the student body is on partial- or full-tuition scholarship) makes it possible for students from low-income families

Top: Science class in a newly outfitted classroom. As the science offerings became more sophisticated, the laboratory space had to keep pace.

Oval: Miss Espinosa at a faculty-student basketball game in 1965

Below: The senior flag for 1964

to attend as well….The racial mix includes Blacks, Orientals, Persians, Latin and Mexican Americans. But the majority of the student body is Caucasian."[13] Castilleja at this time was still notably lacking in diversity—and its ongoing efforts to create an inclusive community that enjoys diversity in every sense of the word continues now in the twenty-first century.

America in the late 1960s experienced dizzying changes. Students were caught in a swirl of confusing issues and changing social standards. The class of 1966 marveled at how much had changed during their time in high school: "Memories will flash occasionally—of the apple man who told many of us about Dallas one November day; of the astronauts who flew while we weighted [sic] in our desks as always, knowing that nothing could go wrong because it never did in the movies; of the vague missile sights [sic] in Cuba and the sudden, confusing introduction of a Mr. Kosygin and a Mr. Brezhnev."[14] The world was changing

around the students, but they were changing too. When polled by the *Laurel* in the fall of 1969, 45 percent of students believed marijuana should be legal, although half of those would restrict it like alcohol; 92 percent were against the Vietnam War, and 68 percent had held that position from the start; 76 percent said that if a political issue conflicted with their "moral convictions," they would "work through existing channels" to change things, while 8 percent would "resort to violent means" and 16 percent would "remain uninvolved"; 73 percent wore miniskirts most often; 51 percent liked a boy's hair to be to his collar, and 24 percent wanted it even longer.

The increasing awareness and activism of the student body matched California and national trends. The change from the 1950s was striking. Miss Espinosa proved surprisingly understanding and adaptable, mitigating the clash of generations. Even as she was about to retire, Miss Espinosa could still appreciate youth and understand when changing times called for changing policies: "I am often asked how the changes in attitudes of youth have affected the school program. My reply is that, as always, there is endless variety in the attitudes

of youth, and all of us, old and young, reflect the society in which we live. As far back as I can recall, youth has had its special vocabulary and craved many of the trappings of age, and I remember having seen at least a half dozen unique dress conventions through the years. Our girls of 1970 are wearing a different uniform; resident seniors have smoking, off-campus, and dating privileges, and supervise their own dormitory during daytime hours; all seniors have the freedom of the campus during study hours. In general, students in all classes have what older alumnae would consider a more relaxed program. There are some more significant changes, however, changes understandable in the light of today's world, their awareness of social needs and concerns, and the fact that life demands that they make judgments at an earlier age....Nevertheless, the girls of 1970 and 1941 have much in common. We still observe an interest in traditional activities, such as the Christmas Pageant, warm response to Founder's Day and Graduation Exercises, and enthusiasm for the more light-hearted aspects of school life."[15]

Indeed, despite significant changes in the world, and even in what Miss Espinosa allowed students to do or encouraged them to discuss, her insistence on tradition, manners, and decorum continued. Ethel Meece, hired in 1968, remembers, "One day, immediately after she had asked the blessing, she taught us how to eat an orange. First, she placed it on a small plate. Then, with a tiny serrated knife, she cut through the skin just enough so that innumerable crescents could be pulled apart—daintily, juicelessly, of course. 'The orange never touches the table,' she announced."[16]

Rules continued to be important, and the Castilleja viewbook from the late 1960s devoted a page to "The Castilleja Community" that explained the need for "certain limitations upon individual privilege" in a "harmonious school community." Regulations regarding "academic achievement, good manners and good taste, school uniform, the school day, the school year, and, for residence girls, schedules for visiting, telephoning, free and closed weekends" were considered "necessary if the school is to assure continuance of the standards which lead parents to select Castilleja for their daughters."[17] In case that elegant explanation was not enough, the *Castilleja*

"The increasing awareness and activism of the student body matched California and national trends."

Top: Singing and playing at the 1968 banquet

Oval: Miss Espinosa pouring tea in the residence parlor

"Never has it been more necessary that learning be related to life."

School Handbook for the late 1960s took no chances. It stated that "girls are not permitted to wear exaggerated 'hair-dos' or makeup when in uniform" and banned the "possession, use, or evidence of use" of "marijuana" and "L.S.D."[18]

Miss Espinosa brought up school rules with the Mothers' Club in 1965. She said that, although the school had many methods of communicating with parents, the same questions continued to arise. She pointed out that the "greatest causes for complaints are: transportation, homework, grading, curriculum (desires of girls for different courses), and discipline. These are the same in every school… but it is the responsibility of the school to keep channels of communication open to *all* parents."[19]

In a changing world, Castilleja helped the girls make the necessary transitions. Class Day continued to celebrate achievement in all areas of school life. Castilleja rewarded high academic and athletic achievement, much as it has in every era. In addition to the individual achievement of being on the honor roll, the Scholarship Cup was awarded to the class with the "highest number of girls on the honor roll throughout the year."[20] In 1972, the Castilleja Award, the school's highest honor today, was created to celebrate the girl who best embodied all five Cs. The first recipient was Nancy Jane Ditz '72.

The school continued on its grand plan to rebuild every building. The dedication of the new library and Rhoades Hall, named for longtime trustee and Board Chair Dusty Rhoades, took place on November 9, 1967. Addressing the school on this occasion, president emeritus of Mills College, C. Easton Rothwell, said, "Today we dedicate a beautiful and functional new building. This building, in which living has been so wisely and graciously combined with learning, is both a part of Castilleja's future and a symbol of it. Never in our history as a people has it been more important that living be informed by learning. Never has it been more necessary that learning be related to life."[21]

Having seen Castilleja through the 1960s, Miss Espinosa felt ready to retire, noting that "the times pointed to the need for a young principal once more."[22] Her retirement was not a surprise to the Board; she had given them five years' warning. "Thirty years is long enough to

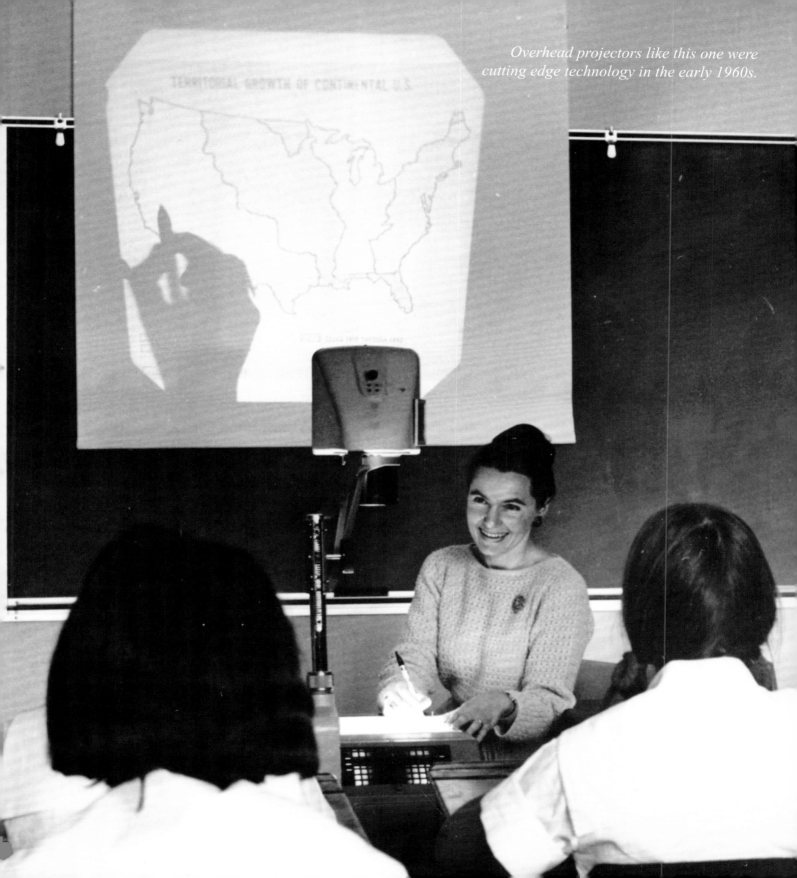

Overhead projectors like this one were cutting edge technology in the early 1960s.

Mrs. Meece, Mrs. Wahlborg, Miss Hackvate, and Mrs. Hermenau having tea at the 1971 Junior-Senior Banquet

be in one place," she said, and "I really don't want to run anything anymore."[23] Donald R. Westmoreland's appointment as her successor was announced to the Castilleja community in the summer of 1970, but he did not begin his work until July 1971. This year allowed the Castilleja community to get used to the idea that Miss Espinosa was leaving. She surprised many with her decision to join the Peace Corps. In her work at Ewha Women's University in Seoul, South Korea, Miss Espinosa showed again how to lead by example and work hard for the improvement of women's education. After her return to Palo Alto, she became a frequent and proud guest at almost every important Castilleja function until her death in 2002.

Mr. Westmoreland was from North Carolina. He earned a Bachelor's degree from Duke and a Master's degree from the University of Alabama and left his job as headmaster of the Westminster School for Girls in Atlanta, Georgia, to come to Castilleja.[24] In his first address to the school, he assessed the state of the school in its sixty-fifth year and his vision for it: "Beginning in 1907, the faculties and administrations have steered this old ship through two world wars, a depression, a great inflationary period, and the tumultuous sixties, a decade which could be looked back upon in future years as the darkest period of the twentieth century.... Castilleja should be a happy place. It should be a school of flexibility, of humor, of warmth and love. More than anything, it should be an academic institution where each student feels at home and where she counts as a person."[25] The new head had faith in Castilleja and a desire to honor its traditions by investing in its facilities and its faculty.

Mr. Westmoreland worked to whip the school into financial shape. He knew that "Castilleja must build a substantial endowment targeted at specific goals: scholarships, faculty compensation, library acquisitions, sabbaticals, and faculty enrichment."[26] He oversaw the continuation of the large-scale building program that had begun in the 1960s, with the construction of the Seipp-Wallace Pavilion and the Ely Fine Arts Center, the renovation of the Chapel into an auditorium, and many other smaller projects. Mr. Westmoreland knew that a

"More than anything, it should be an academic institution where each student feels at home and where she counts as a person."

great school required a strong faculty, and he worked hard to ensure that Castilleja would attract and retain good teachers. He worked to raise their salaries and was concerned about "the cost of living in the Palo Alto area."[27] Although it might seem to some that every penny raised must have gone into the building programs, in fact much of the increase in expenses went to improve faculty salaries, hire more faculty, and provide benefits such as the faculty sabbatical program introduced in 1979. The program rewarded length of service with a sabbatical semester at half pay or a quarter at full pay for "further study or travel." The first two years of the program granted sabbaticals to some of Castilleja's longest-serving teachers of the time: Hilde Jarman, Margaret Wahlborg, Dorothy Feldmann, Jane Hermenau, and Toni Hsu.[28] Teachers were also rewarded with the new Distinguished Teacher Awards on Class Day. The first awards went to Susan Sheehan and Sherry Rusher. In the 1970s, teachers' base salaries were also raised significantly. Art teacher Loraine Birch remembers being summoned to Mr. Westmoreland's office to discuss her salary. She thought, "Oh no…he must think we all make too much in California" only to be asked, "Why is it so low?"[29] Although he shared common assumptions about women workers not needing high salaries in this era, and he did not want to pay more than necessary, he aggressively went after foundation money and tried to provide incentives to keep the best teachers at Castilleja. He brought the same energy to the curriculum. The number of advanced placement tests taken by Castilleja students more than doubled while retaining a mean score higher than the national average.[30] The foreign language graduation requirement was increased to three years in one language rather than two years of language courses. Among the many new courses were AP calculus and computer programming (in BASIC), using the

The Sixth C: Construction

The construction of the new Residence Hall, completed in 1962, was supposed to be the beginning of an extensive building campaign to replace every building on campus. It took a little longer, however, than the planners had counted on to raise the necessary funds. In addition, the sudden need for a new pool became evident in 1963, when repairs became impossible. The money for that project was raised by a Fathers' task force. The next building in the plan, however, became a reality in 1967, when the new classroom building, Rhoades Hall, opened for use with 20 classrooms and a wide second-floor walkway shaded by two heritage oak trees and affording an excellent view of the Circle. The old gymnasium and the arts building were the next to be replaced. Construction began on the new gymnasium in 1976, and in 1977 the Seipp-Wallace Pavilion opened. The Ely Fine Arts Center, including the Seipp Gallery, named for Anita Seipp '71, opened in 1980 with a show of photographs by Robert J. Steinberg. The final part of this building campaign was a renovation of the Elizabeth Hughes Chapel to include a real stage, wings, backstage space, and in the basement a greenroom, dressing rooms, and a costume storage area.

Top: Students holding a lunch meeting in the Sunken Patio.

Oval: Latin teacher Ann Criswell talking to parents at back-to-school-night in the mid-1980s

school's two Apple computers.[31] Students in the late 1970s continued to enjoy acceptances to America's finest colleges. Alongside these changes came new concerns about "academic pressure."[32] Amanda Kovattana '76 remembers, "What did define us were our grades...Those who made the honor roll had their names called in chapel and got to stand up."[33] A "joint faculty-student ad hoc committee" was formed "to study extensively academic demands at Castilleja."[34] Although Mr. Westmoreland was "concerned," he did note, "The problem of academic pressure seems to be a national one. And the 'pressure' as such seems to be more of a pressure for good grades. For the first time since the 1950s, the pressure seems to be more evidenced by internal and peer pressure than attributed to school or parents."[35]

Many adults who worked for Castilleja look back on this period as one of building for the future. Penny Black, initially a math teacher and later the first Dean of Students, looked back on these years and recalled the dedication of everyone involved: "In contrast to every other school where I have worked, I remember the tireless work of the Board of Trustees. When I arrived,

the new classroom buildings had been finished under the leadership and sponsorship [of]... Dusty Rhoades. Bette Moorman was the head of the Academic Committee and worked constantly to ensure that our students and teachers participated fully in the learning process. I went with Don Westmoreland at the suggestion of Ed Seipp and Leonard Ely...to evening get-togethers to talk about the need for a new gym and art facilities. These three did so much to further the academic, physical plant, and fiscal growth of the school."[36]

But the greatest achievement of the period lies in a change that was not made. Single-sex education was increasingly unpopular nationally, and when surrounding schools merged or went coed, it was even harder for girls' schools to compete. A member of the class of 1976 remembered her matriculation at Castilleja this way: "Outfitted with secondhand uniforms and donated books, I took my place in the school at a time when girls schools were still considered relics of a bygone era."[37] By the 1978-79 academic school year, there were only 551 girls schools in the country, fewer than half as many as there had been in 1965-66.[38] But Castilleja held strong.

In 1981, Mr. Westmoreland stood up for all-girls education: "With the rapidly developing opportunities available for women in every professional area, it is very important for girls to have the best possible academic training for college. The opportunity to hold positions of leadership at every level and the chance to be competitive on athletic teams which have full use of athletic facilities are essential. I was visiting with a headmaster of a school…that had gone coed a few years ago, and I asked him about the girls basketball team. His reply was 'We don't have a girls' team—the boys' teams are using the gym so much that there isn't a place for the girls to practice.' I believe students in a girls school are truly first-class citizens, and should think of themselves as such…If anything, a single-sex school makes more sense today than it ever did."[39] Nancy Ditz '72 credits a group of powerful men on the Board of Trustees with the determination to keep Castilleja a single sex school. "Every time I see Ed Seipp, Len Ely, my dad, and Rev Wallace, I thank them…. They knew in their hearts…that Castilleja should stay single sex."[40]

Castilleja continued to enjoy traditional activities, such as the Christmas Pageant and the Maypole Dance, but some things were changing. A member of the class of 1977, the first class not to have known either Miss Lockey or Miss Espinosa, noted, "Traditions that we had witnessed as younger students changed, or were even abolished, as we progressed through the years: the Ruffians and the Raiders [and] the over-the-top nature of Junior-Senior Rivalry week. Instead, the school tried to be hip and modern, offering exchange classes with Menlo [for a very short time], weekend exchanges with RLS, and 'groovy' classes like Human Sexuality and Personality."[41] Class retreats were the descendants of the picnics at Alum Rock, weekend trips to Hidden Hollow, and ski weeks at Yosemite. Sophomores went to the Yosemite Headland's Institute in Marin County. Biology teacher Mrs. Meece and several other sophomore teachers accompanied the girls as they studied ocean tide pools and coastal habitats. Each May, the senior class enjoyed a retreat at Asilomar on the Monterey Peninsula for a "last opportunity for the class to be together." By the end of the 1970s, the freshman class would also go to Asilomar to get to know one another

The choir for the 1969 Christmas pageant poses by the Christmas tree.

at the beginning of high school as the retreat program expanded to include all Upper School grades.[42]

Castilleja struggled to find its place in a transformed world. Its purpose was still to educate girls and prepare them for the future, but their options were much broader than they had been before. Girls could now attend Ivy League schools and were encouraged to aspire to have both a career and a family. This may have been an era of streakers and speakers on sexuality and cult deprogramming, but the 1970s also had a conservative backlash to the previous decade, and Castilleja, too, sent mixed messages to its students. Upset by the "cataclysmic social disruptions of the '60s," Verna Stewart spoke at the 1979 Founder's Day, "exhorting young women to *consider* a career as a housewife and mother."[43] On the other hand, the school tried to accommodate the needs of working mothers: on Parents' Day in 1976, the earliest appointments for conferences with teachers were reserved for "fathers and working mothers," while the rest of the day was divided alphabetically by the student's last name.[44] And it was, as English teacher Nancy Flowers remembers, a "big deal" when Mr. Westmoreland said at the end of the 1975-76 school year, "I am happy to announce that you ladies may now wear pant suits to school."[45] Earlier contracts had specified that female teachers had to wear dresses, heels, and hose. Mr. Westmoreland often reminded students to behave: "Remember, girls, be guided by dignity and honor."[46]

The school's expectation that students should work hard, think hard, and not pay attention to anything other than college was difficult, if not impossible, to maintain for some girls when they saw what was going on around them. Amanda Kovattana '76 remembers a particular disconnect with American history in the mid-1970s: "What I had experienced of the United States was a military presence in Southeast Asia that pretty much implied that Americans went anywhere they wanted and did what they wanted."[47] She remembers one class that seemed to fit with her brain and her ideas about the world, an experimental film analysis class taught by Richard Johnson. Administrators may have felt that they were giving students the world by offering a few such experimental classes, but Castilleja students, like those all over

Top: Mrs. Feldmann and Laura Ware Nethercutt '79 at Commencement in 1979.

Oval: Sally Hutchenson '72 Nancy Ditz '72 and Lucy Baldwin '72 at the Junior-Senior Banquet in 1972.

Top: Members of the class of
1979 dressed up to show their
senior spirit.

Oval: Muriel Anderson '79
and Lynn Anderson '78

"Castilleja
has provided
much of the
confidence and
inspiration by
which we have
learned to use
our minds."

the country, did not want to give administrators credit for small changes; they wanted bigger changes.

In her valedictory address, Cynthia Norton '78 summed up what Castilleja had given her class. Although she mocked the "valuable guidance" they had received, "from the first warnings against the evils of jeans, shorts, and halters, and of excessive male companionship, to the recent suggestion to refrain from hurling graduation bouquets at the audience," she concluded with a more serious observation: "Castilleja has provided much of the confidence and inspiration by which we have learned to use our minds."[48]

This combination of satirical affection for the school and appreciation of the excellent educational opportunities encapsulates the conflicting attitudes of students in the 1970s. Many students had a positive experience, and families who sent their children to Castilleja were pleased with the school. But some students felt that the school was not open to them, their ideas, and their differences. Erika Lim '77 put it bluntly when she looked back on her experience: "I actually had a miserable time at Casti..." She was a scholarship student and said that the school "never let me forget that."[49]

Although many alumnae have pleasant memories from the era, Castilleja fell victim to the shocks and disruptions of an age with a generation gap that resembled a chasm. The same feelings that alienated students from Castilleja generated high sales for bumper stickers that said "Question Authority" and "Don't Trust Anyone over 30." But even in this rough period, Castilleja stayed true to its core values, and, when many of these students look back on their Castilleja education, they respect the rigorous academics. Ginny Eversole Contento '79 remembers: "Though I was not a stellar student myself, being surrounded by such a commitment to excellence couldn't help but rub off, even decades after actually attending the school. I am SO grateful for that, as it firmly planted in me a desire to always be better, never get complacent."[50] When alumnae of this era see Castilleja today, most of them like the changes and appreciate that the school has maintained its high academic standards and dedicated teachers while finding ways to become more accepting of difference, more open to the richness of diversity.

GUEST SPEAKERS

"That's what we are here to do, to try to make your journey faster and easier and more joyful and more full of fun and poetry and dancing and seriousness and accomplishment."
—Gloria Steinem, *speaking to Castilleja students*

World-renowned speakers have graced the Castilleja stage in recent years. A 1983 gift from the Morris family began Castilleja's annual tradition of and commitment to excellent guest speakers. The Arrillaga family began another endowed program in 1989. The school is fortunate to have these two endowed funds that bring several exceptional assembly speakers and occasionally a performing arts group to campus each year. After addressing the school, the speakers often spend additional time with students in a small-group setting. Parents and faculty members have also arranged for outstanding visitors to speak at assemblies and graduations. Although recent speakers have drawn much attention, Castilleja in its early years hosted luminaries as David Starr Jordan, first lady Lou Henry Hoover, and efficiency expert Lillian Moller Gilbreth. The following list is a sample of the many outstanding speakers who have visited Castilleja. Asterisks denote those pictured.

Mohammad Yunus*	Jane Goodall*
Jean-François Rischard	Tobias Wolff
The Peking Acrobats	Amy Tan
D.R. Metha	Anna Eshoo
Meg Whitman	Robert Hass
Al Gore	Sarah Wallace '73
Thomas Friedman	Doris Kearns Goodwin
Firoozeh Dumas	Mary Pipher
Minnijean Brown-Trickey	Isabel Allende
Kavita Ramdas	Condoleezza Rice*
Wendy Wasserstein*	Danny Glover
Lori Andrews	Jehan Sadat*
Madeleine Albright*	David M. Kennedy
Queen Noor	Maya Angelou*
Chicago Symphony Players	Fran Leibowitz*
George Shultz*	Loretta Green
Lalita Tademy	Pauline Kael
Joyce Maynard	Nien Cheng
Anne Lamott	Martha Stewart
Sally Ride	Dean Butler
Gloria Steinem*	Peter Coyote
Adeline Yen Mah	Ron Suskind
Carly Fiorina	Polly Draper
Claybourne Carson	Lillian Moller Gilbreth
Bob Ballard	Lou Henry Hoover
Richard Rodriguez	David Starr Jordan

SCHEDULE

"All of us at the school are excited about the new schedule which will be called the rotating schedule."
—Donald Westmoreland

Top: Students from the class of 2012 getting ready to go to class

Center: Melanie Mueller '82 reads by her locker.

Below left: The daily schedules for day and residence students in 1938-39

Below right: Like most students, Kelly Kalinske '09 highlighted her schedule and hung it in her locker.

Today, Castilleja students and teachers love and hate the complicated schedule! In the early days of the school, the five academic periods, and required chapel, did not change from day to day, or year to year. As the curriculum became more complicated, additional periods were added to the end of the day for labs, clubs, conferences, and advanced placement courses. The rotating daily schedule started in the middle of the 1971-72 school year. In a letter to parents, Mr. Westmoreland explained the change: "By rotating the daily schedule we will be eliminating the routine of the same schedule every day, thus creating a better learning situation for the students and a better teaching situation for the faculty." Since that time, there have been several major and uncountable minor schedule modifications, each accompanied by extensive discussion. Recently the trend is toward simplification, for example five minute passing periods rather than four minutes, and consistent break and lunch times. But each new schedule has the same goal: the best learning and teaching experience for Castilleja's students and teachers.

Upper School Day Schedule

Opening	8:30 a.m.
First Period	8:30- 9:25 a.m.
Second Period	9:30-10:25 a.m.
Third Period	10:35-11:30 a.m.
Chapel and Luncheon Hour	11:30- 1:15 p.m.
Fourth Period	1:15- 2:10 p.m.
Fifth Period	2:15- 3:10 p.m.
Sports Periods	3:10- 4:30 p.m.

RESIDENCE SCHEDULE

Daily Schedule

Rising Hour	6:45 a.m.
Breakfast	7:15 a.m.
Luncheon	12:15 p.m.
Dinner	6:15 p.m.
Study Hall	5:00-6:10 p.m.
Study Hall	7:25-9:05 p.m.
Lights Out	9:45 p.m.

Kyra McCarty '10 getting something from her friend's locker

Middle School students blowing bubbles on the Circle in 1986.

Chapter Seven
CHANGING WITH THE TIMES

"Along with the true value of friendship, Castilleja has taught us to set goals with a future purpose in mind, to meet those goals, and then set new, higher ones."
—Karen Schaider '84

The 1980s brought changes to the United States, to California, and of course to Castilleja. The decade saw the explosion of personal computers, preppy clothes, leg warmers, CDs, and the fall of the Berlin Wall. The 1980s also saw the beginning of the Silicon Valley technology boom, the first cable TV service in Palo Alto, the presidency of Ronald Reagan, and a generally conservative climate in the United States. By the end of the decade, Castilleja would benefit from some of these developments and be ready for new challenges, thanks to the groundwork laid by Mr. Westmoreland. He invested in both facilities and faculty and ensured Castilleja's academic competitiveness. By the school's seventy-fifth anniversary, Castilleja was ready to "offer the best of the old and adopt the best of the new."[1] The pace of change was quickening, and students, faculty, and administrators learned not just to keep up but to anticipate and lead.

CASTILLEJA AWARD

First presented in 1972, the Castilleja Award goes to the "Castilleja senior who, by vote of the faculty, best exemplifies the qualities of the five Cs: conscience, courtesy, charity, courage, and character." Since 2002, the valedictorian and the Castilleja Award winner give speeches at Commencement.

Top: Karen Tobey works with Stefanie Restifo '86 and Deborah Sicherman '86.

Oval: A student works on a dissection in science.

Below: Artwork from the 1981-82 Student Handbook demonstrates how to make the honor roll.

HIGH HONORS

HONORS

HONORABLE MENTION

Students and faculty understood that the tone and spirit of the times had changed. In her Founder's Day speech in 1989, senior Alison Marston described what English teacher Susan Sheehan (formerly Albro, now Barkan) called her "ultimate litmus-test for girls' philosophies of life": their reaction to the writings of Henry David Thoreau. Mrs. Sheehan had told Alison that as times changed, so had student reactions to the nineteenth-century American author who gave up city life for the solitude of a small cabin on Walden Pond. "During the late 60s and early 70s Thoreau was simply your favorite author. [Students] saw him as a soulmate, an inspiration, the ultimate individualist. In the 80s, [they] see him as, well…a nut. 'He went to Harvard. And he wasted it!'"[2] Times had indeed changed at Castilleja and in the world.

In California, there was another important change for public education: the 1978 passage of Proposition 13, a property tax freeze. While this tax reform was seen at the time to be a people's victory against taxes, its lasting legacy has been to dramatically compromise California public schools, which rely on

property taxes for their funding. Per-student annual spending in California went from hundreds of dollars above the national average in 1978 to well below the national average by the 1990s, thanks mostly to Proposition 13.[3] Independent schools became options as parents realized how much the public schools were suffering. But the infusion of new blood that the influx of students would bring to Castilleja had to be matched by some modifications. Castilleja, like other independent schools, had to change with the times.

The 1980s also saw some significant changes in leadership at Castilleja. Mr. Westmoreland left at the end of 1986. For two years, Jay Milnor served as Interim Head. Jim McManus came in the summer of 1988, and served as Head for five years. Three headmasters in under ten years made this decade a chaotic one for Castilleja. New leadership, however, brought new ideas and energy, which helped the students and faculty develop a supportive and empowering community and helped to ensure that the school was in touch with the times.

If personnel changes in the administration seemed a bit confusing, the same was not true in

One of the first computers used by students at Castilleja was this Apple II.

English teacher Mrs. Sheehan reads Julius Caesar *with Gail Freidenrich '84 and Alison Hawley '84 in the ninth grade.*

Top: Jackie Glynn '85, Karen Mah '85 and Renata Sworakowski '85 work together in French class.

Oval: Heather Allen Pang '84 waits to be called on in Mrs. McKee's Russian history class in 1983.

either the classrooms or on the Circle. Students and faculty kept on doing what Castilleja does best. The dedicated faculty and students worked toward higher understanding and greater knowledge, mastering the subtleties of problem solving, scientific inquiry, and excellent writing. Many alumnae from the 1980s remember how hard they studied for Mrs. Meece's biology tests, how Mrs. Hermenau relived Mrs. Dalloway's day in slides and memories from her sabbatical, how Mrs. Hsu never lost her patience as she went through each point again to make sure everyone understood sine and cosine, how Mrs. McKee paused for students to supply answers ("the enemy of my enemy is my friend"), how Mr. Johnson brought drama into English class and never left English out of drama, how Ms. Coltos (formerly Mullen) exhibited a single-minded devotion to finding that one fact a student sought in the library, and how Mrs. Jeffers and Ms. Bishop guided each senior through the stresses of college applications. These alumnae can also recount with fondness the quirks and trademarks of their mentors: Ms. Rusher's early-morning can of Tab, stories about Effie, the head-huntress, that Mrs. Sheehan used as fodder for grammar lessons, Mrs. Criswell's pretzel dress, M.J.'s friendly wave from her bike, Rudy's excellent food, Mrs. Marston's cheery "good morning, people," and Mr. Westmoreland's formal "we are dismissed" at the end of chapel.

In a 1985 Founder's Day speech, senior Lynne Lampros poked fun at the "close-knit community of Castilleja," remarking that a student "could sneeze in front of one teacher and the next day be asked by another how her cold was." She concluded, "I don't know if I will ever again feel the support, caring, and love from so many people. But I will always remember it."[4]

In the seventh and eighth grades, then called the Lower School, students prepared for high school but still managed to stay young in many ways. Lower School Head Barbara Towner (now Deubert) told of "Life in the Lower School" in 1984: "The girls' Lower School curricular program provides them with a strong foundation for high school subjects, an emphasis on study skills and organization techniques, and...a love of learning." In the seventh grade, science was optional but a study skills class was not. Many eighth graders chose to take drama; plays such as *Goodbye, Mr. Chips* and musicals

"I don't know if I will ever again feel the support, caring, and love from so many people. But I will always remember it."

Top: Ms. Towner looks for someone to call on in the Choral Room.

Oval: Students made huge Papier-Mâché food in Ms. Spark's art class. Joyce Kim '94 made this taco when she was in seventh grade.

Below: The cover of the 1984 Mochuelo *was drawn by Rhonda Tierney '84.*

such as *Oliver* were popular. "Because seventh and eighth graders abound in enthusiasm, imagination and energy, each year new ideas are added to the Lower School program."[5] The seventh graders began a long tradition in this period: the Papier-Mâché Buffet. Students in Susanne Sparks' class built skeletons for the huge baked potatoes, hamburgers, popcorn, and pizza and then covered them with newspaper strips. Ms. Sparks reported that "cries of agony began to emerge from the art room; seventh graders were being forced to dip their hands into buckets of gooey wallpaper paste to apply layers of newspaper strips to their still-amorphous foods—to provide strength and smooth surfaces for the forms."[6] Other Lower School activities included Secret Sisters, ice-skating parties, and, of course, dances. In the early 1980s, Ms. Towner and Activities Director Tim Dirks were in charge of dances. As they do today, girls filled out forms with the names of boys they wanted to invite

and listed the music they wanted to hear. Ms. Towner remembers these forms as being full of information—descriptions of the boys as "cute hunks" or "gross nerds" as well as interesting comments on the most popular songs of the moment.[7]

In the Upper School, students longed for more responsibility and independence, asking a sometimes reluctant administration for privileges. Although the school's own self-study suggested that increased independence for students was a continuing goal, progress could not be fast enough for students. Small changes at this time expanded senior privileges, made some minor changes in the uniform (the addition of pants was a good start), and offered an increased role for students in defining rules and discipline. A student group reexamined student government and created the Judiciary Committee in 1984. But students still chafed at some of the traditions, in particular those that carried a religious connotation. Student shenanigans at the 1983 Christmas Pageant, including skipping nuns and a monk wearing a "Groucho" nose and glasses, put the community at odds. Some were angry that the dignity and

tradition of the pageant had been upset while others felt that the pageant was an anachronism. Former Lower School Head Barbara Towner Deubert remembers the death of the pageant: "As I recall, the great deciding factor in eliminating that tradition, and it was time to do that for so many reasons, was the talent show act that the faculty participated in one year, in which we did an irreverent but very funny spoof of the old tradition. In our spoof, the juggler actually dies at the foot of the statue of the Madonna, and an Agatha Christie detective type (played by Jane Hermenau) comes on the scene to investigate what appears to be the murder…It was really so outrageous that the real deal was never performed again."[8]

The event for December 1985 was a Christmas Program. The next December, under the Interim Head Mr. Milnor, the school staged a Festival of Light, with carols, readings from the Bible and Koran, and a menorah lighting. The Festival of Light continued in various forms for a few years before being dropped altogether. Today the Holiday Committee works to see that Castilleja honors the diverse holidays of all the students, faculty, and staff year-round, not only in December.

The Christmas Pageant was not Castilleja's only tradition with religious overtones. On May 29, 1986, thirty-one seniors, led by the co-valedictorians Nancy Allen and Deborah Wallach, signed the following letter to Mr. Westmoreland: "We, the undersigned, feel that the religious nature of the commencement exercises undermines the nondenominational character of Castilleja. Graduation is not a religious occasion, and, therefore, prayer is not appropriate. Furthermore, the idea of the Head of School assuming the position of a religious leader in 'Prayer and Benediction' is offensive to most present. Many beautiful poems could replace the chanted praying, such as 'The Road Not Taken' by Robert Frost. We appreciate the value of Castilleja traditions, but in this instance we feel alteration is in order. We realize that this year's ceremony cannot be changed, but we would appreciate consideration of our objections for future years."[9] The students had called for an important change. The diversity of the student body demanded more points of view, and older traditions that were not inclusive seemed outdated and inappropriate.

Top: Mr. Westmoreland teaching economics in the 1980s

Oval: Carla Crenshaw '80

Top: Baseball on the Circle
in the 1980s

Oval: Mr. Milnor sporting his
classic bow tie and cheerful
smile

Below: Latin project by
Susan Silveira '83

Students took action on other issues as well. In the fall of 1984, Ginetta Sagan, one of the founders of Amnesty International in the US, addressed the Castilleja student body. So inspiring was this Presidential Medal of Freedom recipient that a group of seniors, led by Claudia D'Andrea '84, decided to start a chapter at Castilleja. There were no other high school Amnesty groups on the West Coast and only a handful in the whole country; Castilleja students were pioneers. With the help of their faculty sponsor, Nancy Flowers, they spoke at other local high schools and supported those schools forming Amnesty groups.

By the end of the 1980s there were more than twenty high school groups on the Peninsula.

After 15 years at Castilleja, Mr. Westmoreland resigned, saying, "The time is ripe for a new personal challenge for the Westmoreland family."[10] Chairman of the Board Herman Christensen, Jr., celebrated the accomplishments of the departing Headmaster: "The growth of Castilleja School under his leadership of fifteen years is a most impressive one. Enrollment has grown from 198 girls to 335; the resident student body from 27 to 62. Endowment has increased from $27,795 to over $2,500,000. The Seipp-Wallace Gymnasium and the Leonard W. Ely Fine Arts Center have been built and the Chapel/Auditorium expanded and renovated—all paid for from donated funds. Today, the Castilleja physical plant is valued at approximately $15,000,000… This is a faculty which insists on high academic standards, yet is dedicated to helping each student reach her individual potential in a warm, caring atmosphere."[11]

Laura Arrillaga '88 now wishes she could thank Mr. Westmoreland "because he was the first adult that I had encountered in a professional environment who treated me like an adult. Even though I was the youngest person on the Student Council (I was in eighth grade, the lower school representative at the time), my ideas were as valuable as anybody else's."[12]

Because Mr. Westmoreland announced his resignation in the middle of the school year, the Board chose Mr. Milnor as the Interim Head until Castilleja could complete a national search for a new head. The

Students share a magazine in the residence in the early 1990s.

Stephanie Diaz '93 and Ayanna Cage '93 eating outside in the sunken patio

Princeton graduate had been head of Pomfret School in Connecticut as well as Robert College in Istanbul.[13] In the summer 1986 *Quarterly,* Mr. Milnor introduced himself to the school: "Interim appointments provide a special kind of challenge and opportunity. By their very nature they fall within a limited timeframe and goals and objectives must accordingly be cut to fit that cloth. In thinking about the coming year, however, I see no reason to alter some basic principles and interests which have been part of my educational baggage for a long time." He emphasized academics, particularly English, the fine and performing arts, positive peer interaction, and service, as well as "the need for fun, not just satisfaction, relief, or a sense of accomplishment, but plain old fun." He concluded that "if we together can take some modest steps toward these goals, then my hopes and aspirations for the year will have been realized."[14] According to history teacher Mrs. Marston, Mr. Milnor maintained a strong sense of perspective: "Whenever anyone brought up a problem he thought was low level and maybe not worth sweating buckets about, he would say, 'I think this is a problem of dogs in the dining room.'—meaning give it a rest, not that serious."[15]

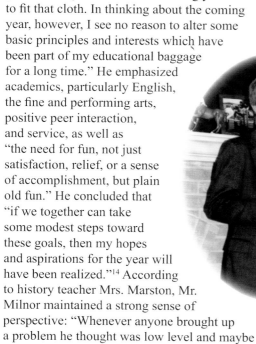

Some of the changes under his tenure included the new English elective program introduced in the fall of 1987 and the first Grandparents Day on April 14, 1988. Mrs. Tobey recalls Mr. Milnor: "He was a grandfatherly type who loved the students. Out to greet students every morning, you could find him 'feeling the pulse' of the campus by interacting with students at all levels. He was famous for introducing a call-and-response greeting that students still know. Many an alumna could finish the phrase he asked before each assembly— 'How do you feel?'—with a loud and invigorating, 'We feel good; oh, we feel so good, uhhh!' A decisive man with strong opinions, people knew where he stood, whether they agreed with him or not. He especially loved the seniors, believing that they were role models to all other students. 'As the senior class goes, so goes the school." Thus he gave special attention to them, nurturing

Top: Mr. Johnson directs Alexandra Dumas '88, Remy Lipkin '86, Kristen French '87 and Steve Bass from a neighboring school in Scenes from American Life.

Oval: Lori duTrieuille '88

them as leaders.'[16]

His successor was also a nurturer, a man who wished to foster girls' development as whole people in a socially responsible school. It took almost two years to find him, but finally the Board selected Mr. McManus to start in July 1988. The new Head held degrees from Occidental and Claremont graduate school and came to Castilleja from Mayfield Senior School in Pasadena. One of his greatest gifts to the school was assembling the "badly needed"[17] Long-Range Plan that was "the basis for the direction that the school headed during his tenure." Indeed, his skills at "planning and facilitating," in addition to his "compassion and eloquence," made him an able administrator who would later consult with independent schools in "creating long-range plans and delineating roles of school administrators, faculty, and board members."[18] By the end of his tenure, his accomplishments at Castilleja included the "codification of scattered procedures" and the "reinstitution of traditional student regulations."[19]

Mr. McManus knew that Castilleja had very strong academic offerings, so he focused on making sure the students were being nurtured as complete human beings who fit with the rest of the world. He came to the school at a point when important discussions and decisions had been put off, and he felt his role was to facilitate the decision-making process. Teachers of the era describe him as "a real humanist" and "an egalitarian."[20] He always wanted Castilleja to foster both "academic *and* personal growth."[21] He was praised for "opening…Castilleja to the larger community, indeed, to the world."[22] He strongly believed in community service and wanted to make it a stronger part of the school: "As a school we stand for something much bigger than mere college preparation—although that is important. We are educating human beings and we owe it to our students—since they are whole people—to work with questions of human values, because those are the big issues when they are out there in the world."[23]

Under the leadership of history teacher Mrs. Tobey, Castilleja had its first Community Service Day on October 9, 1991. This day, taken out of the daily routine to give back to the greater community, was wildly successful: "Inspired by the exceedingly positive impact the

Top: Students brought the 1988 presidential campaign to campus with displays and debates.

Oval: Mrs. Meece prepares for a biology lab.

Below: Students pet the bat ray on their 1991 field trip to the Monterey Bay Aquarium. Julie Packard '70 has directed the aquarium since it opened in 1984.

Driving around the Circle continues to be a favorite treat for the seniors.

volunteer service had on the Castilleja students involved, the faculty voted to implement a community service graduation requirement starting in 1992-93."[24] Castilleja also became more environmentally conscious. With Project STAR, Castilleja began a recycling program and, in 1990, was proud to be Styrofoam free.[25]

Castilleja faculty and students worked to protect the earth and give back to the community. At the same time, Mr. McManus wanted Castilleja to reflect the greater community; he was a strong advocate of diversity. Board Chair Penny Howell recounted his accomplishments at the end of his tenure: "When Jim arrived, the student body was already beginning to be diverse. During his tenure it has become more so, socioeconomically and ethnically, in accordance with a critical component of the Long-Range Plan. He has helped make Castilleja's face blend well with the modern face of California, with sensitivity to the oldest and the newest constituencies and traditions."[26]

In the early 1990s, Castilleja continued to be both a safe and an empowering place for girls; this was especially important at a time when girls' schools were regaining popularity,

thanks to new research into the ways girls learn and the benefits of single-sex environments. One area that saw significant change was athletics; the Board negotiated with the city and the neighbors for the creation of a new field, named Spieker Field, in place of a portion of Melville Avenue. This had been a longtime goal of the school, and it became possible only with the purchase of the Green property, between the existing tennis courts across Melville Avenue.

All these changes helped the student body feel happy about their school. The school alumnae magazine noted "a positive tone in the student body (an observer commented that the students own the school)."[27] Reflecting on her first semester at Castilleja, freshman Amy Chow '96 said, "I really like the warm and friendly atmosphere surrounding the high academic standards here."[28]

Jeannine Marston teaching history

The Sixth Graders Are Coming Back

For 55 years there were Sixth Graders at Castilleja.

Now, after 30 years absence, they are coming back, in the Fall of 1992

Sixth Graders in 1926 at Castilleja School

Applications now being accepted for Sixth Grade at Castilleja.
Castilleja School, 1310 Bryant Street, Palo Alto, CA 94301
Jill Lee, Director of Admission and Financial Aid
Sue Ferguson, Assistant Director of Admission
415-328-3160

Top: Mr. McManus, Miss Espinosa, and members of the Board of Trustees inspect the progress on the new athletic field.

Center: Flyers advertised the return of the sixth grade to Castilleja.

One more big change came to Castilleja in the early 1990s: the return of a sixth grade class. Sixth graders were added for many of the same reasons that they had been dropped approximately 30 years before: to match local schools' grade configurations and to "facilitate academic and personal growth for our students."[29] The announcement that sixth graders would return to the Circle noted that "with the Palo Alto Unified School District having completed this fall its transition to a middle school configuration that includes grades six through eight (an arrangement which mirrors both the local and statewide trends in the recent past), Castilleja needed to decide if it should follow suit." The article also pointed out that the Board did not wish students to have to attend "three schools in three consecutive years."[30]

Castilleja also took note of the trends in educational theory: "American educators in the late twentieth century have reached a broad consensus that a three-year period of transition from childhood to adolescence offers distinct advantages over those of a two-year period. It gives middle schoolers a place of their own, avoids making them elementary schoolers for too long or high schoolers too soon, and it allows a program to develop which has integrity and distinctiveness. In addition, the work of Harvard professor Carol Gilligan—featured not long ago as a cover story in the *New York Times Magazine*—has found that beginning around age 11, girls enter a period of life in which their self esteem and their confidence in expressing their views are dangerously eroded, a phenomenon which is exacerbated by the domineering posture that tends to characterize the behavior of boys at that age. As a school for girls, Castilleja is committed to both academic

"As a school for girls, Castilleja is committed to both academic and personal growth..."

Top: Stephanie Rowen '90 working in a computer lab in the basement.

Oval: Ms. Lonergan during her first year as Head of School

Below: Pamela Hawley '87 and another student in the library in the late 1980s.

and personal growth, and adding a sixth grade will allow us to work with 11-year-olds and carry out our mission more effectively."[31]

That mission was more vital than ever in light of the new research into girls' education. Carol Gilligan's 1982 book, *In a Different Voice,* began the national conversation that would culminate in Mary Pipher's 1994 work, *Reviving Ophelia.* The National Coalition of Girls' Schools was founded in 1991. In 1993, Castilleja planned to reserve "faculty meeting and retreat time to look at issues of how girls learn."[32]

At the end of the 1992-93 school year, when the Board took stock of progress made on the 1990 Long-Range Plan, they noted the "establishment of a human development program for sophomores, with an emphasis on ethical dimensions of decision-making, including sexuality and substance abuse," the "establishment (or revival) of the following courses: Finite Math, Ethics, Honors Physics, Environmental Studies, Geology, Music Theory, Public Speaking, Ceramics, Ethnic Voices in American Literature, and Economics," and the "revamping of the Western Civilization class to the World Civilizations and Cultures class." Plans were in the works to add a "non-European language," specifically Japanese, to the curriculum.[33]

In a little over a decade, Castilleja had been transformed from a highly traditional, somewhat intense, and not always supportive school into a dynamic and inclusive learning community. When Mr. McManus resigned to pursue graduate work, the Board organized a national search and then hired Joan Z. Lonergan as the new Head of School. She threw herself into the exciting challenge ahead: preparing the school to educate girls for the twenty-first century.

Eighth graders walking into promotion ceremonies in 1993

Connie Richardson's Spanish class spends a period in the Language Lab in 2004.

TECHNOLOGY

"We are the internet generation. The technology we use transforms overnight—growing, changing, and evolving just as fast as we do."
—2005 Paintbrush

When Castilleja students think of technology today, they envision the more than 400 computers on campus, including three computer labs, three traveling laptop carts, and a fully equipped language lab. These are girls who use a wide range of software and hardware daily, in school for classes and clubs and in their social lives. They are, as some educators have called them, the "net generation," having grown up with computers, the Internet, instant messaging, digital photography, and iPods. But earlier generations of Castilleja students also loved their new technology, including the two telephones installed in the Administration Building in the 1930s, the electric typewriters used in the basement typing classroom, the one VCR on a cart that started Mrs. McKee's collection of videos in the Fishbowl, the first photocopying machine in the teachers' workroom, and the increasingly sophisticated equipment filling the science classrooms. What Castilleja teaches about specific hardware and software is important. But even more important is how students learn to interact with new technology, to face the inevitable challenges and setbacks of each project or program with persistence, creativity, and an innovative spirit. It is this ability that will allow Castilleja girls to be the masters and creators of the technology of tomorrow.

Top left: Kersten Schnurle '06 works on the prototype for the 2007 Gatorbotics robot.

Center left: John Deubert works with Karen Docter '84, Laura Bushnell '84, Jennifer Bates '84, and Sara Whitesides '85 on one of the first computers on campus.

Bottom left: Math teacher Sara Gilliland '94 and students use the first laptops that came to the classroom on a cart for students to use.

Bottom right: Students take typing during World War II.

GRADUATION

"What I perceive before and all around me—your lovely dresses, your crowns of fresh flowers, your faces full of life and joy, the trumpet fanfare and sonorous organ, the choir of voices—all celebrate and affirm the privilege that is this education and the adventure that is womanhood."
—Judy Johnson

Top right: Graduated seniors from the class of 1930 process out of the Chapel after the ceremony.

Center right: Head of School Joan Lonergan congratulates a senior from the class of 1994.

Bottom right: Lilla Hunter, Sue Good, and Blair Walker mingle on the Circle after their 1956 graduation.

Below: Katherine Shaw's diploma from 1926

Castilleja's commencement ceremony has a timeless quality. From the earliest days of the school, Castilleja seniors have donned white dresses and carried red roses to celebrate their final moments as students before being granted their diplomas. Although little has really changed, there have been some alterations to the event over the years. Prayer was excised from the graduation ceremony in 1987, and the morning hymn was dropped from the service in 1991. The graduation for the class of 1993 was the final one to be held in the Chapel; today, the ceremony takes place under a white tent on the Circle. The class of 2002's graduation was another first. It was the first year that graduating seniors did not wear white gloves and the first year that, in place of the salutatorian, the Castilleja Award winner gave a speech accompanying the valedictory address.

Today, graduation is held on a Saturday in early June, and Castilleja caters a reception afterward. An alumna from 1956 remembers that "graduation was on a Tuesday and there was a party in San Francisco afterward. You wore your graduation dress…You hoped you didn't spill." But mostly, Commencement is about celebrating the accomplishments of that year's seniors, as individuals and as a class. Beth Harris '77 remembers that "when we graduated, [Mr. Westmoreland] gave a nice talk and mentioned every girl, and said something about their personalities. I recently found this, and it was very accurate—he talked about someone's quiet confidence, or their exuberance.—I think he actually knew us fairly well."

Castilleja School

This Testifies that
Katherine Blanchard Shaw has completed the studies required for Graduation from this School and is entitled to this Diploma.

In Testimony Whereof, witness the signature of the principal, given at Palo Alto, California, this Eighth day of June, Nineteen Hundred and Twenty-six.

Principal.

Castilleja School
Palo Alto, California

Kerstin Lindstron, Andrea Chin, Brittany Brown, Ashley Schoettle, Rachel Bolten, Amy Walecka, Jennifer DePuy graduating in 2006

Lizzie Raffin '00 on retreat in the fall of her ninth grade year

Chapter Eight
WOMEN LEADING

"Our goal is to prepare girls who will meet their own measures of success, not someone else's; young women who will be leaders in their own lives—confident, clear, passionate, and strong about their convictions, their purpose, and their values—as well as leaders in the lives of others."
– Joan Lonergan

When Joan Z. Lonergan accepted the position of Head of School, she brought Castilleja into the twenty-first century with a renewed dedication to educating young women for the challenges and opportunities in an increasingly digital and globalized world. Ironically, the challenges Castilleja faced at the dawn of the new millennium were hardly different from those Miss Lockey described 90 years before: to prepare girls for "…a world which seems to be drifting socially and economically…." and where "…there is need, as never before, for girls to have an adequate foundation for the problems which womanhood now faces."[1] Ms. Lonergan framed Miss Lockey's vision in modern language with the school's new motto, Women Learning, Women Leading. Under her leadership, Castilleja

TIE CEREMONY

On the first day of school, new students are welcomed to campus. The faculty pin red carnations on the seniors; the seniors cross the Circle to tie the green ties on the 9th graders; the 8th graders cross the Circle to tie the yellow ties on the new 6th graders; any new students in other grades have their ties tied by their big sisters. Finally, the bell rings to summon everyone to a short assembly in the Chapel.

has rebuilt its facilities, renewed its commitment to fostering every kind of diversity, established student voice and leadership as school-wide priorities, and integrated state-of-the-art technology into the classroom. The school continues to give young women a world-class education that prepares them for the nation's elite colleges and creates opportunities for students to grow into their roles as leaders in the community and in the world.

In the early 1990s, a spate of publications on how girls learn coincided with a renewed interest in girls' schools. Subsequent discussions focused on leadership and empowerment for girls. As part of Castilleja's mission to foster articulate leaders with the courage to act on their convictions, the school adopted a new, and somewhat daunting, graduation requirement: the senior talk. Despite the added stress, everyone—even the seniors—agrees that these five-minute speeches, delivered in the Chapel Theater to the entire Upper School, have enriched the school community and given each senior the opportunity to speak publicly on an issue of importance to her. Reading through

any year of senior talks illustrates the wide range of seniors' interests, feelings, passions, and talents. For example, in 1997, girls chose to talk about living in foreign countries, the importance of family, AIDS, racism, their frustration with or love of Castilleja, the uniform, the dorm, the death of a grandparent, diversity, computers, internships, community service, summer camp, the senior lounge, Internet chat groups, chocolate, sexual orientation, dance, the Holocaust, friendship, and breast cancer. While themes come and go, each year seniors delight the school with their knowledge, their humor, and their passion. In light of the success of the senior talks, the Middle School added the eighth grade speech as a graduation requirement in 1998. The class of 2001 was the first to give eighth grade speeches; since then, each eighth grader, like each senior, has described her hobbies, ideas or interests to her fellow students and her teachers. When looking back on the first two years of senior talks, then Dean of Students Ellie Dwight reflected that they "have had us laughing, crying, and almost always reflecting." She added that although the experience of public speaking challenged some, most seniors valued

Erin O'Malley '10, Sherri Billimoria '10 and Caroline Abbott '10 working in robotics in 2007

"We want them to leave here with the confidence that they can not only survive public speaking, but also thrive in the process."

the experience. She said, "We want them to leave here with the confidence that they can not only survive public speaking, but also thrive in the process."[2] Ms. Lonergan, echoing other heads, often reminds the seniors that they are the leaders of the school, and "as the seniors go, so goes the school." The senior talks have made that kind of leadership prominent. This new requirement was indicative of Castilleja's desire to find new ways to empower its girls to find their voice at a time when many educators worried that most girls were losing theirs. During the 1990s, students began to run school and class meetings, create new clubs, serve on the Judiciary Committee and generally take much more prominent role in shaping all aspects of student life.

When Ms. Lonergan arrived in 1993, she needed to implement the 1990 Long-Range Plan and respond to the pressures of fundraising. Castilleja, like other independent schools, had suffered enrollment problems in the 1980s, as the last of the baby boom generation graduated. While many schools had made the decision to abandon single-sex education, others—including Castilleja—determined to reinvent girls education.[3] A group of independent schools formed the National Coalition of Girls' Schools (NCGS) in 1991 to promote girls schools as a modern solution to the educational needs of girls. Castilleja became a charter member of the coalition, joining "with other respected girls schools across the country who believe that an organization of girls schools with professional leadership promoted girls schools more prominently and effectively than each school can do individually—make the case, do research, and support member and start up schools."[4] Castilleja continues to be an active member, and Ms. Lonergan currently serves as the vice president of NCGS.

Good schools not only maintain and improve their physical plant but also examine and assess new pedagogies and educational advances. In 1991, the Western Association of Schools and Colleges (WASC) visiting committee recommended that Castilleja systematically incorporate pedagogy based on new research to address issues of women's ways of learning. This topic became important nationally in the early 1990s with the publication of the AAUW report "How Schools Shortchange Girls," Carol Gilligan's

Top: Although enrollment in the residence program declined, the girls there formed life-long friendships as they lived and studied together.

Oval: Helen Ashton '07 runs track in 2004.

Below: Juniors and Seniors show their class colors (purple for juniors, red for seniors) during Rivalry in 2004.

In a Different Voice: Psychological Theory and *Women's Development*, and Mary Pipher's *Reviving Ophelia*. In 1997, Castilleja's WASC self-study addressed the ways in which this new awareness had changed both the curriculum and the pedagogy at Castilleja. The study stressed the importance of collaborative learning and the expansion of topics about women. Significant opportunities for student leadership and independence, such as peer tutoring and teaching assistant programs, came out of this research, as did the increased focus on developmentally varied and appropriate teaching methods.

A major change came to the Castilleja campus in the early 1990s—the end of the boarding program. Although the 1990 Long-Range Plan supported the continuation of the residence program for Upper School students, it recommended reviewing the program regularly "to ensure that it possesses the integrity, vitality, and financial viability required to justify its continuance."[5] This same plan outlined the phasing out of the boarding program for seventh and eighth graders "to better serve the needs of Upper School resident students."[6] During the fall of 1993, the administration hired a consultant and formed a committee to examine "the educational and philosophical, not monetary, contribution of the dorm to the school."[7] The boarding population was declining; the boarders were about 11 percent of the student population, but they used 30 percent of the facilities. Recruitment had become increasingly difficult in a time when applications of day students were rising. After careful analysis of all the available information, the vote of the Board of Trustees was unanimous to phase out the residence program over three years so all current boarders could graduate.

Students, especially residence students, reacted emotionally to the process and the decision. They expressed concerns that the loss of the dorm would limit the ethnic diversity at Castilleja, since many of the boarders came from Hong Kong, and make the school less homey. Sharon Gerbode '97, a five-day boarder, reminisced about her life in the dorm in her senior talk: "I had twenty eight new sisters and a crazy, lovable dorm-mother named Janet who would always be there for me…. The dorm became my life. The relationships I developed with the dormies became my source

of stability...We did not view the dorm...as an ugly building with a moody heating system and carpeting from decades ago; we saw it only as home."[8] When the decision was announced in chapel in early 1994, two dorm students spoke about their feelings, "We are here, then, not to oppose the closing of the dorm, which is already decided anyway, but to express our shock and anger and sadness."[9] The decision to close the residence program was not an easy one, but a declining boarding population made it necessary. Many alumnae still mourn the loss of the dorm, however necessary or practical the choice was.

The possibilities opened up by phasing out the residence program helped create the present outstanding campus facilities. In 1996, the renovated residence became the Arrillaga Family Campus Center, which included expanded department and faculty work space, the new Margarita Espinosa Library, classrooms and a new lab for languages, offices for student publications, a new senior lounge, offices for college counseling and community service, and, perhaps most significantly, space for three computer labs and offices for technology staff.

The former language classrooms became the new science wing, and the library and old senior lounge were completely remodeled to create Middle School classrooms and offices.

Realizing the potential created by the end of the boarding program required significant fundraising. Fortunately, Ms. Lonergan has been a dynamic force in soliciting generous and heartfelt financial support for the school. The Program for the 21st Century (P21) raised over $22 million and funded new goals in learning, teaching, and leading. The generosity of the school's supporters did not stop with new buildings and technology: faculty compensation, endowment, and scholarships were the outcome of Castilleja's successful P21 campaign. It took a decade of hard work, but by 2002 the campus had been transformed. Parent John Arrillaga brought his leadership and his generosity to the efforts; as Ms. Lonergan said, "With his support the Program for the 21st Century had more than legs: it had wings."[10] Program co-chairs Penny Howell and Denny Crimmins led the drive with the support of such Castilleja parents as Alan Austin, Bill Friedman, Nicole Orr, and Tom Tisch.

Ms. Lonergan reminded donors, "I believe that the truly dramatic changes in education are going to take place in independent schools....There is no better place than Castilleja to take the big steps toward true innovation."[11] With support for increased technology, improved facilities, expanded financial aid and salaries, Castilleja was truly ready to move into the twenty-first century.

Creating space for computers was only the first step in bringing technology into the school and the classroom. By 1993, new campus uses of technology at Castilleja were omnipresent. Chemistry students in Doris Mourad's class used a laser disc player and a 27-inch television to access a database on the elements. Students publishing *Paintbrush, Counterpoint, Flame,* and *Mochuelo* used PageMaker 5.0 on a new LC520 with a CD-ROM drive. Sixth graders made Hypercard stacks in history and learned to type more than 20 words per minute. And in the library, CD-ROM databases for research and one computer connected to the Internet allowed students and faculty to participate in the very beginning of the information revolution. Two years later, there were over 100 computers and 30 printers on campus, and the *Castilleja Quarterly* published the school's first e-mail address: Info@castilleja.pvt.k12.ca.us.[12] The school had 180 computers on campus in the 1996-97 school year, and Motorola donated 100 more the following year. Significant gifts from the Bechtel Foundation, the E. E. Ford Foundation, Silicon Graphics, and many parents, alumnae, and friends helped bring Castilleja along with hardware and software.

Summer technology grants for the faculty, started by parent Larry Kelly, made it possible for teachers to learn how to use this equipment in the classroom to enhance teaching and learning. By 2006, there were more than 400 computers on campus, including three computer labs, three mobile laptop carts, and laptops for most faculty and administrators. Now there are LCD projectors in every classroom, and "digital photography and filmmaking have moved from the novel to the commonplace. More and more students may be found in computer labs working on multimedia projects."[13] The library Web site includes access to online databases, the card catalogue, citation guides, and much more. Eighth grade U.S. history

"There is no better place than Castilleja to take the big steps toward true innovation."

students make documentaries, students studying design learn Adobe Illustrator, and students taking Spanish, French, modern East Asian history, and African Studies build Web sites. The first goal of Castilleja's 2000 Long-Range Plan was to "exploit technology to enhance our students' education."[14] Although this goal might ever remain a work in progress, Castilleja students and faculty are increasingly making technology an important tool in the learning process.

The creation of a distinct, developmentally appropriate, carefully articulated Middle School program of academics, arts, wellness, clubs, and athletics was another important development of the 1990s. The return of sixth graders in 1992, the end of the residence program, and the renewed focus on how girls learn best all came together to support a reconfiguration of the Middle School into a place that would meet the "developmental, curricular, and pedagogical challenges" of girls in the sixth through eighth grades.[15] When Anne Cameron came to Castilleja as Middle School Head in 1996, she emphasized the particular needs of Middle School girls;

they "have unique needs distinctly different from elementary and upper school students. They have entered a sometimes intense period of growth and change academically, socially, physically, and personally."[16] In 1997, the school formed a Middle School task force of faculty, administrators, trustees, and parents to define how to build a Middle School that would "best serve the need of girls in grades six through eight."[17] The Middle School has grown to four sections in each grade and established an identity separate from the Upper School. One of the most significant new Middle School traditions is the Washington, D.C., trip for eighth graders. On these trips, students have met Representatives Nancy Pelosi and Anna Eshoo, Senators Barbara Boxer and Dianne Feinstein, Secretary of State Condoleezza Rice, and Attorney General Janet Reno. Students have seen for themselves what "Women Leading" can mean in politics. Middle School student government takes an active role in making student life enjoyable. Traditions such as Penny Wars to benefit the Red Cross, decorating lockers, Spirit Days, and eighth grade big sisters for sixth graders all reflect the

Becky Chan and Alissa Fletcher playing volleyball against St. Mary's in the 2004-05 season.

The Sixth C: Construction

Castilleja girls often go to class to the sound of construction, and the recent decades have been no exception. Campus construction boomed in the 1990s, starting with the creation of Spieker Field, which replaced the tennis courts and part of Melville Avenue. The construction of the Arrillaga Family Campus Center out of the old residence building and the new science wing and middle school out of one section of Rhoades Hall modernized technology and laboratory space. The Campus Center was named in honor of the late Frances Cook Arrillaga, former trustee, and her daughter, Laura Arrillaga '88. The character of the old building was maintained in the rebuilding of the Gunn Family Administration Building, while space was added and everything was modernized as part of the Program for the 21st Century campaign. This same fundraising drive made it possible to renovate the Chapel Theater. The new Okawa Pool, all deep with eight lanes, opened in 2001 for swimming and water polo, thanks to the work of Diane Guinta, Dorothea Nawas, Joan Stevenson and Heidi Singhoff Brown '74. In 2006, the old gym came down, and, in 2007, the new Fitness and Athletics Center, with twice as much space and modern fitness and athletic facilities, will rise out of the 35-foot-deep hole in the ground to open in the fall of Castilleja's Centennial year.

energy of the Middle School. Changes in the academic program, such as the elimination of grades in the first quarter for sixth graders and first-semester final exams in almost all Middle School subjects, reflect the continuing faculty efforts to provide developmentally appropriate instruction and assessment for Middle School girls. Sara Kauffman '06 looked back from the perspective of college and reflected on her Castilleja education: "These memories are so vivid to me and the skills I acquired even in middle school are still so valuable. I am constantly recounting the concepts learned, discussions had, and papers written in these classes. Not a day goes by on this campus when I don't implement a skill that Castilleja taught me."[18]

New scientific research about the educational needs of girls and changes in the world economy spurred changes in how Castilleja prepares students for adulthood. Ms. Lonergan and John Gunn, Chair of the Board of Trustees, saw that students needed to become global citizens in order to thrive and lead in the twenty-first century. The school's mission statement said in part, "The school blends a contemporary global perspective with a challenging traditional curriculum that prepares students…for college as well as for fulfilled, constructive lives."[19] Changes in the curriculum reflected this expanded focus. Cultures and Civilizations became the ninth grade history course for the 1997-98 school year, replacing the beloved but Euro-centric Western Civilization. In the next years the curriculum developed rich ethnic and global perspectives with African Studies, International Relations, Latin American history, Japanese, Ethnic Voices in America, Asian Literature, World Religions, and Mandarin Chinese (replacing Japanese in 2006).

Although the list has changed over the years, the last decade has seen a significant increase in the global academic offerings at Castilleja.

Student travel and exchanges have been part of the Castilleja experience since Miss Lockey allowed a travel company to come to campus to advertise European trips for students in the 1920s. In the 1980s, summer travel to Europe and Latin America was popular, and the trend have expanded to cover the globe. School-sponsored travel to Egypt, Mexico, England, Italy, Puerto Rico, Cuba, Japan, France, and other locations have broadened

"the school blends a contemporary global perspective with a challenging traditional curriculum"

Top: Eighth graders examine the Vietnam Memorial in Washington, DC on the 8th grade trip.

Oval: Lindsey Austin '98 and Athletic Director Nancy Martin at the Gator Gathering in 1996.

Below: Jaipur Foot Factory founder D.R. Mehta and Eryl Barker in science and Laura Docter Thornburg '81 working with students in Cultures and Civilizations during Global Week 2007.

student experience and knowledge of the world beyond the Circle. The Coltos-Criswell Travel Fund, created by Latin teacher Ann Criswell and Librarian Eleni Coltos on their retirement in 2000, has helped to finance travel for students. Community service clubs and projects have reached out around the world. The exchange program with Junshin, a girls' school in Japan, began in 1996. Each year, girls from Junshin have enjoyed their visits with host families, and every few years, Castilleja students have gone to Japan on summer trips. Exchange students, mostly from Eastern Europe, in the late 1990s brought their different perspectives to the Castilleja community. These steps to increase the global component in Castilleja's program laid the groundwork for the Centennial global program launched in 2005.

As Castilleja became part of the emerging global culture in the 1990s, the school promoted awareness and acceptance of diversity locally. Like many independent schools, Castilleja worked to balance the competing demands of the parents, students, alumnae, faculty, staff, and the community. In 1996, junior Candice Sullivan-Speare wrote an entry for the KRON–*San Francisco Chronicle*–sponsored Diary Project, a compilation of diary entries from teenagers around the Bay Area. She described her experiences being raised by a lesbian couple and the discrimination she faced before coming to Castilleja and finding here "a place where she and her family were accepted and embraced."[20] She read her diary entry at Upper School meeting, and the local press covered the event. Reactions were mixed, and the debate about how Castilleja should be covered in the press turned into a discussion of free speech, diversity, and the rights of gays and lesbians. Ms. Lonergan met with concerned parents to make the school's position clear: "Castilleja supported the right of each student to speak freely at the school, and embraces the diversity of its student body and community."[21] The trustees composed a strong statement supporting diversity that evolved into an official Diversity Policy, which continues to be widely circulated

Top: Patricia Pietrzyk conducts students singing the national anthem before a San Francisco Giants game in 1997.

Oval: Tomi Amos '06 and Elena Marinelli '06 on the Middle School softball team in 1999.

and published with Castilleja's Mission Statement.

Student clubs such as the Rainbow Alliance, Asian Club, Student Nation, Black Student Union, and "PRISM" Indian Culture Club, educate the community about different cultures and perspectives. These students have worked with the Holiday Committee, the faculty, the Assembly Committee, and the administration to make sure Castilleja lives up to its own stated policies. For two years ending in the summer of 1999, the diversity task force, made up of parents, trustees, alumnae, faculty, staff, and administrators, surveyed the Castilleja community and explored ways to live the "Commitment to Understand, Recognize, and Enhance Diversity" that was part of the Diversity Policy. The diversity task force concluded, "The 5 Cs: Conscience, Courtesy, Character, Courage, and Charity—the founding philosophy of Castilleja—represent an ideal mechanism to encourage students to build a sense of shared purpose and pride in the Castilleja community."[22]

Reflecting on the focus on diversity, an article in the *Castilleja Free Press* in 2002

reminded students, "If we complain about the school's focus on diversity, it is only because we are lucky enough to belong to a community where the acceptance of all people, regardless of their race, religion, sexual orientation, ethnicity, or anything else, is so natural as to be taken for granted."[23] On the issue of diversity, students took Women Leading seriously and pushed for actions they felt were important.

As the 1990s went on, Castilleja encouraged students to take responsibility as leaders and innovators. The school hoped to instill in them a sense of independence and an entrepreneurial spirit to prepare for life's challenges. As Elizabeth Yin '00 put it, "Castilleja has a high tolerance for new ideas and thoughts. If you're interested in starting something new at Castilleja, you can usually just hop to it with a little guidance and a lot of work."[24] For example, in 1999, a group of students decided that Castilleja needed a second outlet for student opinions and founded the *Castilleja Free Press*. CFP advisor Joseph Mitchell recalled that, "They wanted to create a publication that could be both informative and editorial in nature and could address politics

"On the issue of diversity, students took Women Leading seriously"

Physics teacher Tim Lynch demonstrates with a hammer, a brick, and his own hand for students from the class of 2005.

Top: Students heading to the Chapel for an assembly.

Oval: Math teacher Camilla Lau listens to Megan Brown'11 during Global Week 2007.

in particular."[25] The publication was popular with students, but the founders' hard work was rewarded with more than just praise. They discovered "an interest that...blossomed into a career goal."[26]

With more student involvement in every area of Castilleja, faculty and parents worried about increased pressures and time demands on students. The 1990s continued the dialogue on student stress and prompted discussions that led to limiting the number of AP courses students could take, eliminating the senior research paper, de-emphasizing awards, and closely examining how students spent their time.

Whether Castilleja students were starting a club, writing a syllabus for an independent study, designing a Web site for their own community service project, making a public service announcement, or giving a senior talk, they demonstrated time and again their independence and creativity. In her senior speech, Courtney Carter '97 summed up her Castilleja education, "Something that most Castilleja students have in common is their ability and willingness to take risks. This may be due in part to the all-girls setting or it may be for other reasons, but students all over campus are trying something new. Some are joining a team for the first time, others are auditioning for their first play, and others are dressing in a red cape and pink pants as Super Peer Tutor....Castilleja has prepared us to take...important risks."[27]

As part of the expansion of student opportunities, Castilleja created an internship program and expanded the offerings of Career Day. On Career Day, sophomores visit a wide range of companies, government offices, and institutions. The internship program provides juniors and seniors with opportunites over spring break and summer to work closely with a mentor and explore a particular field. The program includes regular meetings to compare experiences with other interns and reflect. Castilleja students have visited and interned at a wide range of places, including Lucile Packard Children's Hospital, KQED-TV, IDEO, Adobe, Menlo Park city government, Palo Alto *Weekly,* ALZA, Hands on Medicine, the Institute for the Future, Silicon Graphics, U.S. Geological Survey, Webcor, US District Court, El Camino Hospital, TheatreWorks, and *San Jose Mercury News.*

> *"Something that most Castilleja students have in common is their ability and willingness to take risks."*

Top: The Circle has invited students to read outside since Miss Lockey brought the school to this location in 1910. This photo was taken during the 2003-04 school year.

Oval: Ms. Lonergan and Dayna Li in 2004

"Castilleja was awarded the Commissioner's Cup, which recognizes the best athletics program in the West Bay Athletic League"

Another way students experienced more freedom and the responsibility that goes with it was a significant expansion in senior privileges. Seniors have non-uniform days every Friday in the third quarter and every day in the fourth quarter. When Susan Finlayson '97 reflected on her feelings when she put on the uniform for the last time, she used those feeling as a metaphor in her senior talk for what Castilleja had taught her. "…It has taught me how to NOT be there—how to ditch this joint, as nice as it is, and go out into the world as an educated, liberated woman. Castilleja is not like the rest of the world in a lot of ways… [but] I suggest that Castilleja's other-worldliness can be an asset. Wearing uniforms every day isn't a practice for life after graduation; it has been, for me, a unique way of creating an atmosphere in which I could discover the unimportance of clothing and realize that I am able to tackle life no matter WHAT I'm wearing. More generally, Castilleja has given me the kind of haven and support I have needed to encourage me to adventure confidently out on my own."[28]

Castilleja students continue to assume leadership roles and responsibilities—for example, in athletics. New sports teams illustrate growing student interest in sports and competition. In 1995, there were 15 sports offered, 9 for the Upper School and 6 for the Middle School. By 2004, Athletic Director Jez Mcintosh had increased the total to 20, 12 in the Upper School and 8 in the Middle School.[29] Upper School sports include basketball, cross-country, golf, gymnastics, lacrosse, soccer, softball, swimming, track and field, tennis, volleyball, and water polo. In 2005-06 72 percent of the student body participated in the after-school athletics program. Middle School sports include basketball, soccer, softball, swimming, tennis, track, and volleyball and water polo. The Middle School athletics department has a no-cut policy, allowing all students to play without regard to previous experience or talent. The emphasis in the Middle School program is inclusiveness, while the emphasis in the Upper School is competitiveness. Both programs have shown success at many levels. Between 1998 and 2006, Castilleja teams have won 18 league championships, made numerous Central Coast Section (CCS) appearances, and won 9 CCS Championships.

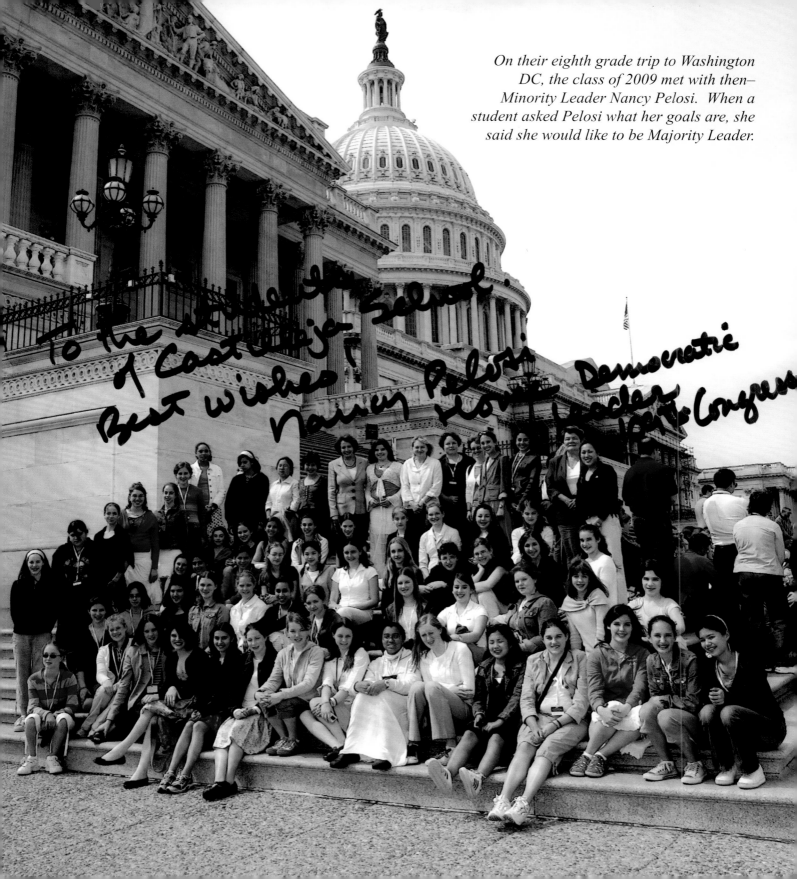

On their eighth grade trip to Washington DC, the class of 2009 met with then–Minority Leader Nancy Pelosi. When a student asked Pelosi what her goals are, she said she would like to be Majority Leader.

THINK OUTSIDE
THE CUBE

MATHCOUNTS

Neli Jasuja '10 works on a
math problem for her class.

$$s \times t = d$$

	s	t	d
bee	70	t	$70t$
2 trains	50	t	$50t$

2 trains meet
they are going

$t \rightarrow$ is the
length of
time it
takes for
train B & the
bee to meet

$70t + 50t = 10$

$120t = 10$

$t = \frac{1}{12}$ hrs.

For the last four years, Castilleja was awarded the Commissioner's Cup, which recognizes the best athletics program in the West Bay Athletic League. Recently, Castilleja has seen the signing of NCAA nationally recruited athletes: Ariel Baxterbeck '06 to Northwestern for volleyball, Stephanie Smith '07 to Santa Clara for softball, and Tori Anthony '07 to UCLA for track and field. With the completion of the new Fitness and Athletics Center in 2007, the program can grow even stronger.

With regard to the visual and performing arts, Castilleja set out "to ensure that the fine arts receive the financial and institutional support necessary to flourish within the overall life of the school."[30] The renovation of the Elizabeth G. Hughes Chapel Theater gave students and teachers a state-of-the-art facility, and productions have thrived. Again, Castilleja students have taken a leadership role to augment the school production calendar. Two seniors from the class of 1996, Emily Glenn and Cara Cipriano, produced and directed a full-scale production of the zany musical *Ruthless,* whose run had to be extended because of popular demand. The students took the proceeds of the

healthy box office and bought the school its first wireless microphones, used for many years in musicals that followed. The Foolwise Players, a brainchild of Paz Hilfinger-Pardo '04, is a drama club that produces student-directed, all-girl productions of plays that are part of the English curriculum. Past productions include *Romeo and Juliet, Pygmalion,* and *The Importance of Being Earnest.* Students have taken the lead in an annual 24-hour play project in which several student production teams spend one Friday night and one whole Saturday to writing, casting, directing, and performing a group of ten-minute plays.

Since its opening in the early 1980s, the Anita Seipp Gallery has been a formidable force for teaching and learning, providing a space for the students to present their work to the public together with internationally recognized professional artists. Students see the importance of the arts in their education and in their lives. Under the curatorship of Deborah Trilling, Castilleja has exhibited a segment of the AIDS Quilt, documentary photographs from Amnesty International's work in Guatemala, photographs by Galen Rowell, and metal work by

Top: Samantha Chang '10 swimming in 2005

Oval: Emma Southgate '10 and Kalena Geissler '10 in eighth grade history class in 2005

Below: This planner belongs to a ninth grader and shows her assignments for the week of September 19, 2006.

internationally recognized artist, Harriete Estel Berman. Because of the gallery's nonprofit status and well-earned stature in the community, it has been the sponsor of numerous grant recipients including local artist, Kathryn Dunlevie, and Castilleja alumna Meredyth Wilson '95.

Around the turn of the century, the visual and performing arts department added photography and filmmaking to the curriculum. Aided by state-of-the-art technology, students at all grade levels and across the curriculum were not only creating photo portfolios and movies but learning to integrate these skills into their work in all of their academic classes and becoming increasingly media savvy.

In her senior talk about dancing, Sara LaBoskey '98 reflected on the importance of the arts in student lives. "Castilleja believes in its students and challenges us everyday to go beyond what we may believe is our best in order to reach our highest potential academically. This requires an endless amount of hard work, and sometimes this work can become draining.

I think it is important to find some form of art through which to channel your emotions and have a chance to focus on something besides tests and essays."[31] In 2004, the Upper School government created the new position of arts coordinator to facilitate communication about the arts for students.

Performing arts and community service came together to produce Dancing for a Difference, which became Arts with a Heart, a benefit for Save the Children performed collaboratively with students from Eastside Prep. This annual event, currently a benefit for Room to Read, combines dance, music, film, and theater around an annual theme, all with a goal to raise consciousness and money for a worthy cause. These performances show the energy with which Castilleja students throw themselves into performances and their dedication to helping others.

Student groups and individuals have used their creative energies again and again in recent years to create their own opportunities for community service. New clubs and projects conceived and run by students include the China Books Project, Project Baobab, Shoes for Ethiopia, Girls for a Change, Youth

As a teaching assistant in sixth grade history, Erin Hill '06 helps Sarah Shore '12 with a project.

Sonali Mehta '11 as Reno Sweeny and Tobi Amos '11 as Billy Crocker in the Middle School musical Anything Goes *in 2007*

Philanthropy Worldwide, Stand Strong against Genocide in Darfur, Nets of Love, and Coats for Kashmir. Ashley Schoettle '06 created Nets of Love to respond to a specific problem she saw on a summer study program in South Africa. She raised money to buy insecticide-treated bed nets to send to women's health clinics in Africa to help prevent the spread of malaria. The Upper School Community Service Award was renamed in 1996 to honor the late Frances Cook Arrilllaga, Castilleja trustee and mother of Laura Arrillaga '88, as an example to students of a lifetime commitment to service. Castilleja's community service program, including Community Service Day, the new community service reflection, the proliferation of student-led projects, and plans for significant service activities during the Centennial Celebration show how deeply ingrained service is in the Castilleja community.

One has only to drop by the reception area and peruse the *Castilleja in the News* binders to see how Castilleja girls spend their time outside school. They compete in Friends of Millard Fillmore (FOMF), robotics, technology, writing, and math competitions. More years than not, the Castilleja team wins first place in FOMF after an exhilarating and somewhat crazy weekend in the Castilleja library and all over the Bay Area looking for clues. Students are also actors and dancers in local performances, social activists in their communities, and athletes of the week in the local paper.

As Castilleja students involve themselves in a myriad of activities, they are often pulled in different directions. Faculty worry about the tendency to go "over the top": banquet decorations that might involve three floors or a Rivalry Week that includes elaborate and costly campus decorations. In an age of competition and competitiveness, Castilleja teachers and parents saw the need to address student stress. In 2004, Castilleja joined a collaborative organization based at Stanford called Stressed Out Students (SOS), in order to understand and lessen the levels of stress. Faculty explored strategies to make their classes, especially homework, developmentally appropriate and reasonable. Through grade-level coordination, exam restructuring, and schedule adjustments,

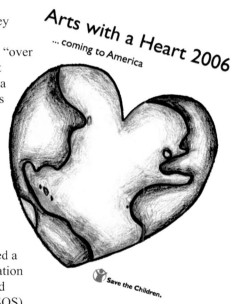

Arts with a Heart 2006
... coming to America

Save the Children.

"No other school could have prepared me better for the rigor of college."

they work to maintain academic rigor and a reasonable student workload. The new schedule and calendar adopted in 2005 provide more study and conference time during the day. On the other hand, alumnae comment on the Castilleja experience positively. Sharlene Su '05 wrote to one of her teachers, "Castilleja demanded a lot of work but the teachers were always committed to enabling students to reach their full potential. Teachers regularly devoted extra free time to helping students. Many of my teachers even scheduled weekend study sessions before AP tests! My friends at other schools were always taken aback by the incredibly supportive intellectual atmosphere at Castilleja when I described it to them. The classes at Castilleja had the perfect blend of support and challenge. No other school could have prepared me better for the rigor of college."[32] Castilleja, with the help of SOS and input from parents and students, continues to help students manage their workload and their outside activities while maintaining the high academic standards that are essential to the school's mission.

Castilleja traditions continue to evolve, and as a few older ones such as the May Fete and the Fashion Show are no longer relevant, new ones come to take their places. On the opening day of school 1993, Castilleja inaugurated a new, and now beloved, tradition: the tie ceremony. Faculty pin a red carnation on each senior, and then the seniors tie the new green ties for the ninth graders. Eighth graders tie the yellow ties for their sixth grade "little sisters." More recently, Ms. Lonergan brought back an old tradition, with the return of the Castilleja C pin for every student to indicate she is an alumna from her first day at Castilleja. Other traditions, such as Baccalaureate, have come from the students. Seniors in the class of 1994 wanted some part of the graduation celebrations to be more student focused. One of the organizers, Thea Marston '94, remembers, "We often felt that Castilleja was not always a school that represented us, but we were happy that we had the opportunity to contribute a tradition that we feel had the potential to represent ALL members of a class and appreciate that the administration was open to a student-planned event related to graduation."[33] Rachel Friedlander was the first Baccalaureate speaker, and the class of 1994

chose Ms. Bishop to be their faculty speaker. Rachel remembers, "It was the only event that we (my class) organized ourselves—it was the beginning of a new tradition…that really meant something to us."[34] The class had some trouble getting approval from the Palo Alto fire marshal to use candles, but they managed it in the end, and the candlesticks were their gift to the school to help continue the tradition. The class of 1995 used the evening for a reading, in pairs, from Dr. Seuss's *Oh, the Places You'll Go!* and for student performances; Assistant Head of School Nancy Hoffman '76 was the faculty speaker, and the class created a slide show illustrating their senior year. Since then, the senior class makes Baccalaureate a celebration of their Castilleja years. This event celebrates the class as a whole and recognizes the end of their journey together.

In the twenty-first century, as in the previous 100 years, the daily rhythm of the school is punctuated by timeless traditions. Some of these include sunning on the Circle, Ringee/Ringer antics, bake sales, theme dress-up days, student-faculty basketball games, senior doughnut sales, weekly Time Clock updates, and being asked "How do you feel?" during assembly. More recent traditions—such as the birthday party for Waldo (Ms. Lonergan's black labrador), visits by Kazi the camel (and a menagerie of other animals), Thursday cookie day, the Festival of Antiquity, and reading "stall stories"—are activities likely to be enjoyed by future generations.

Castilleja students continue to excel in academics. They do exceptionally well on advanced placement exams, become National Merit Scholars, and earn acceptances at the nation's best colleges. Outside the classroom, students began participating in the Tech Museum of Innovation's Tech Challenge and the Lego League international robot competition. Students find their passions and their own leadership skills, as well as their academic abilities, in such experiences. Ms. Lonergan tells the story of one sixth grade team's experience in the Tech Challenge. "A team of sixth graders entered the Tech Museum's Tech Challenge a few years ago, determined that their Robot entry would be hydro-powered, in spite of never having a successful "dry" run.

Top: Lauren Dunec '06 on a summer trip to work at the Sri Ram Orphanage in Haridhwar, India.

Oval: Middle School students pull out invasive plants in Half Moon Bay on Community Service Day in 2005.

"your daughters will find their niche, experience failure on occasion, and thrive in this supportive, resource-filled environment."

Undeterred, they kept trying in the hope that it might work. They arrived at the competition in rain slickers and provided plastic ponchos for the judges. At the end of the day, they were awarded a prize for the most spectacular failure and ended up on the 10 o'clock news, smiling triumphantly. My point: your daughters will find their niche, experience failure on occasion, and thrive in this supportive, resource-filled environment."[35] In 2005, Castilleja's FIRST (For Inspiration and Recognition of Science and Technology) Upper School robotics team won the Rookie All-Star Award at the Silicon Valley regionals and advanced to the national championship in Atlanta. Over 30 students worked on the team, using CAD software to program microprocessors and shop tools to build the robot.[36] The Gatorbotics team went to the national championships again in 2006. According to the Web site the students created to go along with their robot, "The personal goal of the Castilleja Robotics Team is to break the stereotypes surrounding female engineers. As an all-girls school, the girls on the team enjoy the process of learning about machinery and tools, and defying the common tradition surrounding the lack of

women in science and engineering. This is why we promote the vision."[37] Inside and outside the classroom, Castilleja students find success.

In 1994, the *Counterpoint* staff tried to encapsulate "The Real Castilleja." They stressed the different opinions girls had when asked about the life of a typical "Casti girl." "IT IS SOOO STRESSFUL!" "I love it!" The article went on to say that there was no one right answer, but that they wanted everyone to understand that classes and sports, the arts, social events, diversity, and even "the ever present stress" were the heart of Castilleja.[38] Gabriella Dentamaro '98 put the issue a little differently in her senior talk: "Although I don't know exactly what I want to do with my life, I do know something far more important: I know who I want to be. I wish like nothing else to become as strong, as intelligent, and as inspirational a person as the teachers I've had at Castilleja."[39] The majority of senior surveys collected each spring mention the importance of the relationship between students and teachers and the impact those relationships had on a student's Castilleja experience. This comment from an anonymous member of the class of 2003 is representative of many

Tori Anthony '07 reading by her locker in 2006

Liz Harmon '08 and Nicole Cox '08

seniors: "I think the most positive thing was the interaction with teachers and fellow classmates. Castilleja fosters an environment where I can be independent but still get the assistance I need. There's freedom but also guidance. Also, the teachers have really challenged me to question everything. That has been incredibly valuable. Instead of just accepting "that is how it is," I have been instilled with a sense of curiosity to always ask why?"[40] Teachers at Castilleja establish lifelong friendships with students and welcome them back to campus to tell their stories.

While many traditions highlight the spirit and energy of Castilleja students, academics remain the centerpiece of the school: Women Learning is not just a slogan. Inside and outside the classroom, students and faculty are dedicated to lifelong learning. During the 1990s, several departments undertook curriculum examination and revision. The math department adopted the innovative Keck curriculum's emphasis on problem solving. Students need to learn how to think mathematically and how to apply the concepts and ideas they learn to problem solving. The science department re-designed the sequence of Upper School science; they worked collaboratively to incorporate the latest research and ensure age- and grade-appropriate pedagogy. This revised order of courses—physics, chemistry, and then biology—reflects more closely the content and skills needed for modern science. Many students take AP courses in physics, chemistry, and biology or one of a wide range of elective courses in their senior year.

Teacher turnover became an issue in early 2001 as housing costs skyrocketed in the Bay Area. Recognizing how vital a stable faculty is to the overall program, the Board of Trustees launched a teacher retention initiative in 2002 to ensure the stability of the faculty and mitigate against high attrition. Full-time faculty and staff members received a $10,000 bonus when they signed their contracts for the upcoming year. The bonus program has successfully lowered the attrition rate among younger faculty and become a model throughout independent schools nationwide. It is almost a cliché, but one repeated yearly by many students, that it is the teachers

Top: During Global Week 2006, students constructed a map of the world using only recycled materials.

Oval: Kieran Gallagher '12 and Mattie Keith '12

Below: Senior quilt made by the class of 2005.

who make Castilleja what it is. In her senior survey, one member of the class of 2003 wrote, "What I am most attached to at Castilleja—what I think I'll appreciate the most as I grow older and continue to remember Castilleja—is the people in my class, my teachers, and the campus itself."[41] Another student in the same class wrote, "I have had wonderful teachers. I have learned and learned and learned. I have never not wanted to go to Castilleja, and I don't want to think about what I'd be like if I hadn't."[42] On a visit back to campus for the 2007 Global Week panel of alumnae, Alison Marston Danner '89 said that the most important thing she took away from Castilleja was "intellectual fearlessness and high standards. My teachers here taught me to pursue my intellectual ideas and themes and the crazy ideas I wanted to think about. I also learned that I couldn't use the passive voice and that I have to be very rigorous about how I write. It wasn't OK to be sloppy."[43] Retaining excellent teachers is a

challenge that Ms. Lonergan and the Board took seriously and resolved successfully by raising $5.5 million in less than a year for additional compensation.

Through the 1990s and the early years of the twenty-first century, Castilleja continued to strengthen its academic program. In its fast-paced environment, students achieved and thrived. Faculty and administrators monitored the rigorous program to accommodate the competing demands of activities outside school and increased participation in athletics and the performing arts. In her Founder's Day speech, Elizabeth Yin '00 put it this way: "At such a place of high academic rigor, no one breezes through Castilleja. Somewhat paradoxically, this is exactly how Castilleja instills confidence. Because things don't always work out perfectly, everyone learns to persevere and brush off disappointments. One walks away from this place, learning the most important life lesson, knowing how to cope with failure and how to deal with success."[44]

Today, as in Miss Lockey's day, the Castilleja sense of community is one of the

most treasured aspects of the school. Although the tragic events of September 11, 2001 brought the community even closer together and did not end the occasional reference to the Castilleja "bubble," the importance of Castilleja girls becoming informed global citizens was underscored as never before. The class of 2005 entered high school in the fall of 2001, and, looking back on September 11, Nicole La Fetra '05 talked about Castilleja's community in her Castilleja Award winner's speech. "Just two weeks into our freshman year, September 11 rocked our worlds. It could have been the worst time to be among a new class, with friends still little more than strangers and those friendships still tentative. Instead, I witnessed a strength I'd never thought possible. Friends, teachers, parents, administration all came together to offer unconditional support. For many of us, it was the first time we saw the true force of Castilleja. We are not a bubble, ephemeral and easily broken; we are a web, endlessly interwoven, stronger than we may appear. We are more than the sum of our parts in what we can accomplish."[45] Castilleja's community comes together in sorrow and in joy and supports everyone.

Castilleja's history is filled with continuity in its core values, as well as constant change to realize those values. "A glimpse into any classroom at Castilleja typically reveals a small group of girls passionately discussing the issues they care about, debating ideas and expressing their opinions candidly."[46] Although this perspective comes from current admission materials, it could have easily been excerpted from any of the viewbooks produced since the founding of the school. Girls who enroll at Castilleja find themselves in an environment in which intelligence, curiosity, and the ability to articulate and challenge ideas are core to the learning experience. They are actively engaged in their education, their school, and their community, and they care deeply about the world around them. This has been true since 1907, and it will be true in another 100 years.

Castilleja's Centennial celebration focuses on several important goals: "To commemorate the century-long impact that Castilleja School has had in the Palo Alto community…At the same time, the Centennial will expand the school's vision to 'beyond the Circle' with

"a small group of girls passionately discussing the issues they care about, debating ideas and expressing their opinions candidly."

Chelsea Ono Horn '06 uses a laptop to connect to Castilleja's wireless newtwork.

programs such as the Global Initiative and a new gymnasium….To attract and engage the greatest number of alumnae to return to campus, celebrate their years here, and learn about the new face of Castilleja….To build the school's local, national, and international reputation as a leader in girls' education commensurate with our vision and motto, Women Learning, Women Leading."[47] The one important Centennial change for students and the future of Castilleja for the next hundred years is the Global Initiative. The introduction of Global Week in January 2006, the addition of Mandarin Chinese, enhanced global awareness and expanded global content in all courses, faculty trips to China and India in the summer of 2006, and plans for student travel to developing nations are only the beginning of the new focus: "beyond the Circle." To facilitate global education, Castilleja hired Heidi Chang as the first Global Director, giving her the mandate to build a comprehensive program for students in all classes. Eventually, as part of the curriculum, all students will travel and experience the world as global investigators, much as faculty members were in China and India.

During the first Global Week, former vice president Al Gore spoke to students and parents about the problems of climate change and global warming. Students studied such issues as women's health, human rights, and immigration through films, guest speakers, workshops, blogging, and breakout discussions. One student commented on the Global Week blog, "Global week was a great idea. I learned so much important information in only four days and… now I see the world differently."[48] The second annual Global Week focused on girls' education, global issues and problem solving, China and India and also brought back alumnae on the final day to highlight the experiences of Castilleja alums engaged in important international work.

Another big Centennial change is the construction of the new Fitness and Athletics Center. After the school year ended in 2006, the Siepp-Wallace Pavilion was torn down, and Vance Brown Construction's crews started digging. The

new facility will include two gyms, one on top of the other, to more than double the space provided for athletics, fitness, and wellness. As Athletics Director Jez McIntosh explains, "We offer young women an outstanding academic foundation that will serve them for their entire lives. Providing the same level of excellence in our physical fitness and athletics programs is a goal that can be achieved by creating a center where students engage in athletic competitions and practices, dance classes, Pilates, or yoga; work out in the fitness center; and attend health and wellness classes— expanding horizons beyond the classroom and strengthening the community as a whole."[49] While suffering through a year without a gymnasium, Castilleja students and faculty anticipate that the results will be well worth the sacrifice. On the first day of school in 2006, everyone on campus received a small shovel pin to wear during the year as a reminder to "dig in" and show support for the school during the year of construction.

With enrollment at an all-time high and admission to the school consistently very competitive, Castilleja enters its second century in a strong position. Castilleja's Centennial celebration will "celebrate our illustrious past and prepare the school for the challenges of the new century."[50] Ms. Lonergan summed it up this way: "We want to give Castilleja students the tools to succeed, to put all the arrows in their quivers, to provide not only equal opportunity but every opportunity. We want them prepared to create a life—not to take a job but to make a job, a career, and a life that suits them; to know themselves and to like themselves; to be confident and ready to be the best they can be. We also want them to be aware that the privilege of such an education has responsibilities and obligations beyond seeking self-fulfillment and self-knowledge. A life well-lived is not a life of individual achievement to the exclusion of community commitment, but a life of connection and service."[51] Women Learning, Women Leading is not just a slogan: it was, and is, a way of life at Castilleja.

Julia Feiler '09, Kelly Kalinske '09, Julia Ransohoff '09, Brooke Taylor '09, Leilani Herzog '09, and Libby Cooper '09 jump off the wall in the Sunken Patio.

Castilleja School Timeline

1907: Mary Lockey opens Castilleja at 1121 Bryant Street on August 19, 1907 with 14 teachers and 68 students in kindergarten through 12th grade. Boys are enrolled in the grammar school.

1910: The school moves to the 1310 Bryant Street campus with the Circle, Recitation Hall, the Residence, and the Bungalow. The cornerstone was laid on April 30th.

1914: First yearbook published.

1921: Orchard House and swimming pool built.

1926: Chapel built and dedicated to Elizabeth G. Hughes.

1930: First gymnasium built.

1930: Miss Lockey is a delegate to the White House Conference for Child Health and Protection.

1939: Miss Lockey dies; Miriam Converse becomes Principal on May 1st.

1940: Sallie Wilson appointed Principal in March/April.

1941: Margarita Espinosa becomes Principal in January.

1942: The school becomes a non-profit institution with a Board of Trustees. Pauline Chamberlain Fisher '20 is the first Chair.

1945: First newspaper for entire study body published.

1948: Boys are no longer accepted to Castilleja's kindergarten.

1953: Kindergarten eliminated.

1958: Grades 1-4 dropped from Castilleja's program.

1961: Fifth grade eliminated.

1962: Sixth grade eliminated.

1962: New Residence dedicated May 24th.

1963: New swimming pool built.

1967: Rhoades Hall and Margarita Espinosa Library open. New Senior Dorm built.

1971: Miss Espinosa retires. Donald R. Westmoreland becomes Headmaster.

1976: Seipp-Wallace Pavilion dedicated July 4.

1980: Leonard Ely Fine Arts Building finished. Chapel renovation completed.

1986: Mr. Westmoreland leaves; Jay Milnor serves as Interim Headmaster.

1988: Jim McManus becomes Headmaster.

1991: First Community Service Day held.

1992: Sixth grade returns to Castilleja.

1992: Community service graduation requirement added.

1993: Joan Lonergan becomes Head of School.

1993: Spieker Field dedicated September 10th.

1996: Arrillaga Family Campus Center opens.

1997: Last dorm students graduate.

2001: Okawa pool opens.

2002: Gunn Family Administration Building opens. Chapel Theater remodeled.

2006: First Global Week held.

2006: Gym demolished and construction begins on Fitness and Athletic Center.

2007: Castilleja's 100th birthday on August 19.

CASTILLEJA
1907 SCHOOL 2007
100
WOMEN LEARNING
WOMEN LEADING

CONSCIENCE COURTESY COURAGE CHARITY CHARACTER

WOMEN LEARNING, WOMEN LEADING

MISSION STATEMENT

Castilleja School educates women by fostering their intellectual, physical, creative, and emotional growth through an exemplary college preparatory experience within a diverse and supportive community.

By blending tradition with thoughtful innovation, the curriculum encourages both individual achievement and collaborative learning. Castilleja's comprehensive program promotes the development of character, compassion, curiosity, and the capacity for effective leadership.

DIVERSITY STATEMENT

Castilleja is first and foremost an educational community. It is the collective responsibility of the faculty, students, staff, administration, parents, and trustees to sustain a framework conducive to learning and to foster behavior built on trust, respect, compassion, and appreciation for individual differences and ideas. All members of the community are entitled to their views, mutual respect, and courtesy. The school will neither disparage any personal or family choice, belief, or point of view, nor condone any expression of intolerance for community members or the school's commitment to diversity. In order to prepare students for the world in which they will live, and in keeping with the Mission Statement, Castilleja School dedicates itself to an open environment in which all people, regardless of race, color, creed, gender, marital status, age, sexual orientation, political beliefs, physical abilities, ethnicity, socioeconomic status, or religion, can thrive.

CASTILLEJA SCHOOL SONGS

Castilleja Song

Music by Josephine Large • Words by Helen Hatch

Growing wild upon the hillside,
Modest flower of woodland ways,
Castilleja, Castilleja,
Gladly now we sing thy praise.
Castilleja, Castilleja,
We sing thy praise.

Dear to us thy crimson blossom
Emblem bright of hope and cheer,
Round thy name shall ever linger
Memories of school days dear.
Castilleja, Castilleja,
Of school days dear.

Earnest workers, happy hearted,
Loyal to the name we bear,
Glad are we to sing thy praises,
Proud thy crimson hue to wear.
Castilleja, Castilleja,
Thy hue to wear.

Our Day with Thee

Words and Music by Latham True, written for Miss Lockey

Our day with thee is but an episode in life.
Yet in the after-years, when tamarisk and jasmine bloom in spring,
Sweet-scented memories return of work and play
and eager comradeship
And choiring organ pipes at evensong;
And of a woman's quiet eyes and crown of silv'ry hair.

ENDNOTES

Chapter One:

1. *Castilleja School Announcement for 1907-1908*, p. 1.
2. Susan Reynolds Rosenberg, University Archives, letter to Chancellor J.E. Wallace Sterling, April 26, 1976 quoting the May 2, 1910 issue of the *Daily Palo Alto Times* which ran a paraphrased version of the April 30, 1910 speech.
3. Mary Ishbel Lockey quoted in Elyce Melmon, "But an Episode…" *Full Circle,* Spring 2002, p. 8.
4. Ilana De Bare, *Where Girls Come First: The Rise, Fall, and Surprising Revival of Girls Schools,* (New York: Tarcher/Penguin Books, 2004), p. 82.
5. Susan Wels, *Harvard-Westlake: 100 Years,* (Tehabi Books, 2002).
6. *Castilleja School Catalogue for 1910-1911, p.* 16.
7. *Ibid.*
8. DeBare, *op. cit.* Ch. 3.
9. *1910-1911 Catalogue*, p. 16.
10. *Ibid.*
11. *Ibid.*
12. *1910-1911 Catalogue,* p. 39.
13. *1910-1911 Catalogue,* p. 15.
14. *1910-1911 Catalogue,* p. 17.
15. *Castilleja School Announcement for 1907-1908,* p. 2. The same wording runs in all of the announcements for this period and into the 1920s.
16. *1910-1911 Catalogue,* p. 16.
17. *1910-1911 Catalogue,* p. 13.
18. Mary Lockey, "Arbor Day Ceremony – Monday, March 9, 1936," Castilleja Archives.

Chapter Two:

1. *Castilleja School Catalogue for 1911-1912,* p. 18.
2. *Views of Castilleja School*, back cover
3. Mary Lockey, *Traditions and History,* October 1930, p. 2
4. Lockey, *op.cit.,* p. 3.
5. Lockey, *op.ci.t,* p. 4.
6. *Ibid.*
7. *Ibid.*
8. Lockey, *op.cit.,* p. 5.
9. *Ibid.*
10. Lockey, *op.cit.,* p. 6.
11. *Ibid.*
12. Lockey, *op.cit.,* p. 8.
13. Lockey, *op.cit.,* p. 9.
14. May Smith letter to Mary Lockey, Stanford, April 12, 1932.
15. Lockey notes. Castilleja Archive.
16. *Castilleja School Catalogue, 1932-1933,* p. 10.
17. Six Week Reports Grade VIII 1915-1916.
18. *Ibid.*
19. "Announcement" to parents of upper school pupils of Castilleja School from Castilleja School, October, 26, 1932.

20. *Ibid.*
21. *Ibid.*
22. *Castilleja School Catalogue,* 1926-1927, p. 15.
23. *Indian, Paintbrush.* 1914, p. 37.
24. 1926-1927 Catalogue, p. 19.
25. 1926-1927 Catalogue, p. 51-52.
26. *Ibid.*
27. 1926-1927 Catalogue, p. 19.
28. 1926-1927 Catalogue, p. 20.
29. *Ibid.*
30. *Ibid.*
31. 1926-1927 Catalogue, p. 16.
32. 1926-1927 Catalogue, p. 11.
33. Ward Winslow and the Palo Alto Historical Association, *Palo Alto: A Centennial History*, Palo Alto Historical Association, 1993, p. 256.
34. 1926-1927 Catalogue, p. 16.
35. 1926-1927 Catalogue, p. 18.
36. *Ibid.*
37. *Ibid.*
38. "Educational Attainment Table A-1. Years of School Completed by People 25 Years and Over, by Age and Sex: Selected Years 1940 to 2004" *Source: U.S. Census Bureau Population Division, Education & Social Stratification Branch,* Maintained By: Information & Research Services Internet Staff (Population Division) <http://www.census.gov/population/www/socdemo/educ-attn.html> Last Revised: March 27, 2005.
39. DeBare, *op. cit.,* p. 51.
40. *Ibid.*
41. *Times* "Stanford Girl First Winner of Pilot's License," December 22, 1928
42. "The Etcher's Art," *San Francisco Chronicle* Rotogravure, Pictorial Section, November 12, 1933.
43. Beth Hughson letter to Helen Henry,1932.
44. Herbert Hoover letter to Mary Lockey. May 26, 1932.
45. *The Stanford Illustrated Review,* July 1932, p. 427
46. *Ibid.*
47. *Ibid.*

Chapter Three:

1. Margarita Espinosa, personal interview, 1986.
2. [Budget Report], 1933-34, p. 1.
3. "Prospects for Re-Enrollment" June 29, 1933.
4. "Prospects for Re-Enrollment" June 29, 1933.
5. [Notes on 1933-34 Budget], p. 3
6. [Notes on 1933-34 Budget], p. 3
7. "Brief Outline of the Financial History of Castilleja School" Feb. 20, 1933, attached to letter from J.F. Prior, Certified Public Accountant, to Mary I. Lockey.
8.. *Ibid.*
9. Notes for Miss Lockey preparing to secure a loan,

1933.
10. "Sophomore Activities," *Indian Paintbrush,* 1935.
11. "Junior Activities," *Indian Paintbrush,* 1935.
12. "Senior Class Activities," *Indian Paintbrush,* 1934.
13. "Athletics," *Indian Paintbrush,* 1934.
14. "Senior Class Activities," *Indian Paintbrush,* 1934.
15. "Senior Activities," *Indian Paintbrush,* 1935.
16. "Senior Activities," *Indian Paintbrush,* 1937.
17. "Freshman Activities." *Indian Paintbrush,* 1936.
18. "The Dance Program," *Indian Paintbrush,* 1934.
19. *Castilleja Circle,* April 1939, p. 2.
20. *Castilleja Circle,* April 1939, p. 4
21. *Castilleja Circle,* January, 1940, p. 5.
22. Margarita Espinosa, "Statement of History of Castilleja becoming a Non-Profit Institution." No Date. Castilleja Archives.
23. *Castilleja Circle,* May 1940, p. 1.
24. Margarita Espinosa, "Statement of History of Castilleja becoming a Non-Profit Institution." *Op Cit.*
25. *Castilleja Circle,* May 1941, p. 2.

Chapter Four:

1. Aurelia Henry Reinhardt, Letter to Mrs. Fisher, April 6, 1942.
2. Margarita Espinosa, "Statement of History of Castilleja becoming a Non-Profit Institution." *op. cit.*
3. Aurelia Henry Reinhardt, Letter to Mrs. Fisher, April 6, 1942.
4. Nana Stevick Wells, *Castilleja Circle,* June 1942, p. 1.
5. Margaret K. Coyle, "Summer Plans at Castilleja," *Castilleja Circle*, May 1943, p. 2.
6. "To the Parents of Castilleja Pupils," February 12, 1943, p. 2.
7. "Freshman-Sophomore History," *Indian Paintbrush,* 1942.
8. Margarita Espinosa, "Letter to Alumnae," *Castilleja Circle,* June 1942, pp. 1-2.
9. Pauline C. Fisher, Letter to the Alumnae of Castilleja School, February 27, 1943, p. 2.
10. "Junior Class History," *Indian Paintbrush,* 1942.
11. Dorothy Zumwalt, "I'm Seeing This War Through." *Indian Paintbrush,* 1945.
12. Shirley Potter, "From the Bomber Factory." *Indian Paintbrush,* 1945.
13. Nancy Clark, "War is Like That." *Indian Paintbrush,* 1945.
14. Margarita Espinosa, "Thirty Years in the Principal's Office," September 17, 1981.
15. "Bwang Bait," *The Laurel,* December 19, 1945.
16. "Bwang Bait," *The Laurel,* February 20, 1946.
17. "Educational Attainment Table A-1. Years of School Completed by, People 25 Years and Over, by

Age and Sex: Selected Years 1940 to 2004" *Source: U.S. Census Bureau Population Division, Education & Social Stratification Branch* using 1952's data for women 25 years old and older. Maintained By: Information & Research Services Internet Staff (Population Division) <http://www.census.gov/population/www/socdemo/educ-attn.html> Last Revised: March 27, 2005.
18. "Class Activities: Senior," *Laurel,* March 6, 1946.
19. "History of Castilleja Enrollment and Tuition Charges," Castilleja Archive File, "Enrollment Figures 1941 on."
20. "Resident and Day Enrollment 1947-1948," Castilleja Archive file, "Enrollment 1942-1953."
21. "Resident and Day Enrollment 1947-1948," Castilleja Archive file, "Enrollment 1942-1953." At least seven boys were in kindergarten that year. Similar documents for the subsequent years show no names that suggest a male pupil. Another report in the Castilleja Archive file "Enrollment Figures 1941 on" says that boys were dropped from kindergarten between September 1947 and September 1948.
22. Margarita Espinosa, *Castilleja Circle,* January 1947, p. 3.
23. Margarita Espinosa, *Castilleja Circle,* December 1949, p. 3.

Chapter Five

1. James S. Fay and Stephanie W. Fay eds, *California Almanac* 4th edition, Pacific Data Resources, Santa Barbara, 1990, p 2.
2. Blair Walker Stratford, interview, June 21, 2006.
3. *Castilleja Paintbrush,* 1955.
4. "Student Court Policies on Citizenships" from file "Student Court – Miss Espinosa."
5. *Ibid.*
6. Blair Walker Stratford, interview, June 21, 2006.
7. Susannah Harris-Wilson, letter to Linda Rafferty, October 10, 2002.
8. DeBare, *op. cit.,* p. 159.
9. "Life Behind the Lace Curtain," *The Laurel,* September 28, 1955.
10. "Life in the Residence," *The Laurel,* January 19, 1954.
11. Barbara Finley, "School Spirit," *The Laurel,* September 28, 1955.
12. Joan Knowles, interview, Summer 2006.
13. Robin Moseley, "Teaching the Culturally Deprived…" *Castilleja Circle,* Spring 1964, p 4.
14. "New Honor System," *Laurel,* November 19, 1953, p. 1.
15. *Parents' Bulletin,* April 1959.
16. *Castilleja Circle,* May 1953, p. 4.
17. *Parents' Bulletin,* December 4, 1957.
18. *Castilleja Circle,* December 1954.
19. Diana Hunter Roth, *Castilleja Circle,* May 1950.
20. *Castilleja Circle,* December 1954.
21. *Laurel,* October 29, 1958.
22. *Castilleja School Prospectus* [1950], p. 3. The same language repeats throughout the 1950s.
23. Blair Walker Stratford, interview, summer 2006.

24. *Castilleja Paintbrush,* 1954.
25. Quoted in Elyce Melmon, "Margarita Espinosa" *Castilleja Full Circle,* Fall 2002, p. 8.
26. "Meet Miss Algeo," *Castilleja Circle,* December 1960.
27. Susannah Harris-Wilson, letter to Linda Rafferty, October 10, 2002.
28. *Castilleja Circle,* May 1958, p. 3.
29. *Parents' Bulletin,* Fall 1953.
30. *Parents' Bulletin,* March 1955.
31. Margarita Espinosa, *The Laurel,* September 28, 1955.
32. Margarita Espinosa, *Castilleja Circle,* May 1951, p. 3.
33. "Have you ever realized how lucky you are to be attending a private school?" *The Laurel,* March 30, 1954.
34. *Castilleja Paintbrush,* 1957, pp. 4-5.
35. *Castilleja Circle,* December 1956, p. 3.
36. "Programs for the Future– Castilleja School." March 11, 1958. To the Board of Trustees. From the Committee on Educational Policy, p.4
37. Margarita Espinosa, Letter "To Parents of Grades I, II, III, IV," March 27, 1958.
38. "Programs for the Future– Castilleja School," March 11, 1958, To the Board of Trustees, From the Committee on Educational Policy.
39. *Ibid.*
40. Programs for the Future 1958, p. 2.
41. *Castilleja Circle,* December 1948.
42. Programs for the Future 1958, p. 4
43. "Out of Present Needs…A Plan for the Future," *Castilleja Newsletter,* March 1960, p. 2.
44. *Castilleja Circle,* March 1962.
45. *Ibid.*

Chapter Six:

1. Cynthia Swanson Miller, interview on Alumnae Day (May 13?)
2. "Casti Forms JSA Chapter," *The Laurel,* April 1965.
3. *Ibid.*
4. *Ibid.*
5. "Asian Crisis Intensifies," *The Laurel,* February 1965.
6. "The Ku Klux Klan," *The Laurel,* November 1965.
7. "Sex Education Debate High Point of J.S.A. League Convention," *The Laurel,* November 1969.
8. Margarita Espinosa, "Dear Alumnae" letter, *Castilleja Alumnae Magazine* 1970, p.12
9. *Ibid.*
10. DeBare, *op.cit.,* p. 167.
11. *Castilleja Paintbrush,* 1969, p. 64.
12. Budd Austin, "Historic Castilleja Geared for Learning," *Peninsula Living,* November 6-7, 1965, pp. 12ff. , *Palo Alto Times*
13. Castilleja School "Self-Study" 1978-1979, p. 3a.
14. "Seniors of 1966," *The Laurel,* June 1966. The strange spelling is in the original, reflecting student humor of the day.
15. Margarita Espinosa, "Dear Alumnae" letter,

Castilleja Alumnae Magazine, 1970, pp. 2-3.
16. Elyce Melmon, "Margarita Espinosa," *Castilleja Full Circle,* Fall 2002, p. 8.
17. Castilleja School *View Book,* no date, [internal evidence suggests it is after 1968 and before 1972].
18. Castilleja School *Hand Book,* [1967-68], p. 30.
19. Castilleja Mother's Club minutes, March 8, 1965.
20. Castilleja School *Hand Book,* [1967-68], p. 18.
21. *Castilleja Circle,* Fall 1967, Dedication ceremony for new buildings November 9, 1967
22. Address by Dr. C. Easton Rothwell President Emeritus of Mills College "The Building of Castilleja's Future", pp. 3-4.
23. Margarita Espinosa, "Thirty Years in the Principal's Office," September 17, 1981.
24. Quoted in Mary Fortney, "New Principal Named for Castilleja School; coming in 1971," *Palo Alto Times,* Tuesday, August 4, 1970.
25. Elyce Melmon, "But an Episode" unpublished manuscript, Castilleja Archives, pp. 29-30.
26. *Castilleja Bulletin* (new publication with vol. 1 number 1 in October 1971) "From the Headmaster— Castilleja: Past-Present-Future" Excerpts from the Address to the Faculty and Staff, September 7, 1971.
27. Donald Westmoreland, *Castilleja Quarterly,* Summer 1981, p. 5.
28. Donald Westmoreland, *Castilleja Quarterly,* Summer 1981, p. 3.
29. Donald Westmoreland, Letter to Alumnae, Aug. 4, 1980.
30. Quoted in Elyce Melmon, "But an Episode" unpublished manuscript, Castilleja Archives, p. 30.
31. Donald Westmoreland, *Castilleja Quarterly,* Summer 1981, , p. 5 and "Why Castilleja" [1974-75] Castilleja Archives.
32. Donald Westmoreland, *Castilleja Quarterly,* Summer 1981, pp 4-5.
33. Donald Westmoreland, "Headmaster's Report to Board of Trustees," May 8, 1979, pp. 1, 3.
34. Amanda Kovattana, "Return to the Bell Jar," May 20, 2006, <http://amandakovattana.blogspot.com/> accessed July 24, 2006.
35. Donald Westmoreland, "Headmaster's Report to Board of Trustees," May 8, 1979, p 3.
36. *Ibid.*
37. Penny Black, e-mail to Jeannine Marston, August 1, 2006.
38. Amanda Kovattana, *op.cit.*
39. DeBare, *op. cit., p.* 172.
40. Donald Westmoreland, *Castilleja Quarterly,* Summer 1981, p. 2.
41. Nancy Ditz, interview, June 21, 2006.
42. Erika Lim, e-mail to Peggy McKee, July 2006.
43. Retreat information from letters to parents from Donald Westmoreland, 1971-1979.
44. Verna H. Stewart, Founder's Day Address, April 6, 1979, p. 2.
45. Donald Westmoreland, Letter to Parents, November 29, 1976.
46. Quoted in Jane Hermenau, "Castilleja Stories" unpublished, Castilleja Archives.
47. Quoted in Elyce Melmon, "But an Episode"

unpublished manuscript, Castilleja Archives, p. 31.
48. Amanda Kovattana, *op. cit.*
49. Cynthia Norton, "Valedictorian Speech," June 7, 1978.
50. Erika Lim, e-mail letter to Peggy McKee, July 2006.
51. Ginny Eversole Contento, e-mail to Jeannine Marston, July 2006.

Chapter Seven:
1. Donald Westmoreland, 75th Convocation Speech Draft, to be given September 17, 1981.
2. Alison Marston, quoted in "Founder's Day Celebration" *Castilleja Quarterly,* Spring 1989, p. 4.
3. Jennifer Sloan McCombs and Stephen J. Carroll, "Ultimate Test: Who Is Accountable for Education If Everybody Fails?" *Rand Review,* Spring 2005, accessed August 3, 2006. <http://www.rand.org/publications/randreview/issues/spring2005/ulttest.html>.
4. Lynne Lampros, quoted in Sinda Mein, "Founder's Day" *Castilleja Quarterly,* Summer 1985, p. 17.
5. Barbara Towner "Life in the Lower School" *Castilleja Quarterly,* Summer 1984, p. 12.
6. Susanne Sparks "Pirates, Patience, Pinafore, Papier Mache" *Castilleja Quarterly,* Summer 1984, p. 14.
7. "Faculty Close-up: Barbara Towner," *Castilleja Quarterly,* Summer 1984, p. 18.
8. Barbara Towner Deubert e-mail to Jeannine Marston August 15, 2006.
9. Letter from members of the class of 1986 to Mr. Westmoreland.
10. Donald Westmoreland, letter to Herman Christensen, Jr., December 10, 1985.
11. Herman Christensen, Jr., letter to "Castilleja Parents and Friends" January 8, 1986.
12. Laura Arrillaga, interview, June 2006.
13. Herman Christensen, Jr., memorandum to the Castilleja Faculty and Staff "Appointment of Interim Head."
14. *Castilleja Quarterly,* Summer 1996.
15. Jeannine Marston, e-mail to Sara Croll, August 16, 2006.
16. Karen Tobey, e-mail to Sara Croll, August 16, 2006.
17. *Castilleja Quarterly,* Winter/Spring 1993
18. Karen Tobey, e-mail to Sara Croll, August 16, 2006.
19. *Castilleja Quarterly,* Winter/Spring 1993.
20. Jeannine Marston, e-mail to Sara Croll, August 16, 2006.
21. *Castilleja Quarterly,* 1991
22. *Castilleja Quarterly,* Winter/Spring 1993.
23. *Castilleja Quarterly,* Summer 1990.
24. *Castilleja Quarterly,* Summer 1992.
25. *Castilleja Quarterly,* Winter 1990.
26. *Castilleja Quarterly,* Winter/Spring 1993.
27. *Castilleja Quarterly,* Summer 1992.
28. *Castilleja Quarterly,* Fall 1992.
29. *Castilleja Quarterly,* Fall 1991.

30. *Ibid.*
31. *Ibid.*
32. "The Castilleja Long Range Plan: An Update on Actions Taken," February 2, 1993
33. Report of The Long Range Planning Committee As Adopted by The Foundation Board, January 1990, p. 16.

Chapter Eight:
1. Castilleja *Viewbook,* undated, probably early 1920s.
2. Ellie Dwight, "Senior Talks," *Around the Circle,* April 1998, p. 4.
3. DeBare, *op. cit.*
4. Joan Lonergan, e-mail to authors, November 2006.
5. "Report of the Long Range Planning Committee," January 1990, p. 19.
6. *Ibid.*
7. Jhumki Basu, "The Dorm Decision: The Student View" *Counterpoint,* March 1994, p. 3.
8. Sharon Gerbode, Senior Speech, *Castilleja Senior Talk Book,* 1997, Castilleja Archives.
9. NaNa Chung quoted in Jhumki Basu, *op. cit.*
10. Joan Lonergan, "From the Head of School," *Full Circle,* Spring 2002, p. 3.
11. "Castilleja's Program for the 21st Century," Campaign Publication. Castilleja Archives.
12. "From the Board Chair," *Castilleja Quarterly,* 1994-95 Review, p. 2.
13. *Around The Circle,* July 2004
14. *Castilleja Long-Range Plan,* 2000.
15. Anne Cameron, "Plans for a New Middle School," *Castilleja Quarterly,* Spring 1997, p. 24.
16. Anne Cameron, "The New Head of Middle School Looks Ahead," *Around the Circle,* Summer 1996, p. 1.
17. *Around the Circle*
18. Sara Kauffman, e-mail to authors, January 2007.
19. "Report of the Long Range Planning Committee" January 1990, p. 3.
20. Joan Lonergan, quoted in Carey Jones, "Castilleja and Sexual Orientation: An Interview with Joan Lonergan" *Castilleja Free Press,* Nov. 2002, p. 20.
21. *Ibid.*
22. Ellie Dwight and Sharon Nelson-Barber, "Diversity Task Force Report," *Around the Circle,* Summer, 1999.
23. Jones, Interview with Joan Lonergan, *op.cit.*
24. Elizabeth Yin, Founder's Day Speech, 2000, Castilleja Archives.
25. Joseph Mitchell, e-mail to author, Jan. 18, 2007.
26. Megan Wilcox-Fogel, Founder's Day Speech 2001. Castilleja Archives.
27. Courtney Carter, Senior Speech, *Castilleja Senior Talk Book,* 1997, Castilleja Archives.
28. Susan Finlayson, Senior Speech, *Castilleja Senior Talk Book,* 1997, Castilleja Archives.
29. "Castilleja Athletics Gains Recognition!" *Around the Circle,* Spring 2005, p. 3.
30. "Report of the Long-Range Planning

Committee" January 1990, p. 17.
31. Sara LaBoskey, Senior Speech, *Castilleja Senior Talk Book,* 1998, Castilleja Archives.
32. Sharlene Su, letter to Jeannine Marston.
33. Thea Marston, e-mail to Jeannine Marston, July, 2006, Castilleja Archives.
34. Rachael Friedlander, e-mail July 2006, Castilleja Archives.
35. Joan Lonergan, Back-To-School-Night Speech, 2004, Castilleja Archives.
36. "Snapshots from Around the Circle," *Around the Circle,* Spring 2005.
37. "About Us" *First Gatorbotics* Accessed 1/2/2007. <http://www.gatorbotics.com/aboutteam1700.html>
38. Ayse Inan and Sonalie Duggal, "The Real Castilleja" *Counterpoint,* May 1994.
39. Gabriella Dentamaro, Senior Speech, *Castilleja Senior Talk Book,* 1998, Castilleja Archives.
40. Senior Survey, 2003.
41. Senior Survey, 2003.
42. Senior Survey, 2003.
43. Alison Marston Danner, "Alumnae Panel" Video Recording. January 12, 2007, Castilleja Archives.
44. Elizabeth Yin, Founders Day Speech, 2000, Castilleja Archives.
45. Nicole La Fetra, "Graduate Speech," June 2005, Castilleja Archives.
46. Castilleja, *Admissions Viewbook,* 2004.
47. "Centennial Celebration" *Full Circle,* Spring/Summer 2006, p. 6.
48. Comment on "Global Week is Just the Beginning" <www.castillejaglobal.typepad.com/11-12a/> Jan. 20, 2006. Accessed January 19, 2007.
49. Quoted in "Fitness and Athletic Center," Castilleja Centennial Campaign, 2006.
50. "Centennial Celebration," Full Circle, Spring/Summer 2006, p. 6.
51. Joan Lonergan, "Joint Trustee and Advisory Council Meeting," November 20, 1996, Castilleja Archives.

ACKNOWLEDGMENTS

Everyone who has ever been a part of the Castilleja community has helped shape the school and its history; we hope you will find your Castilleja here. It has been a joy and a privilege to tell the stories of such a remarkable group of people.

We would like to thank everyone for their contributions to *Castilleja: Celebrating a Century*; some deserve special mention: Our editors Joan Lonergan, Diane M. Allen, Patty Holubar, Jeannine Marston, Peggy McKee, Coralie Allen, Christine VanDeVelde Luskin, Nanci Kauffman, and Susan Barkan have been wonderfully critical and constructive. We have made every effort to check each name and fact. Please forgive any inaccuracies or inconsistencies. Many people pitched in to find photographs, fix photographs, identify people, find quotations, and make this a better book in so many ways. We would like to thank Joan Adams, Alison Marston Danner '89, Elizabeth Leep '81, Maggie Pringle '71, Rachel Bolton '06, Tam Pantane, Karen Weigel, Helen Shanks, Lauren Schryver, David Reichling, Laura Ware Nethercutt '79, Carol Friedman, Cathy Katz, Linda Rafferty, Steve Taffe, Chris Benscotter, and Dennis Galindo. In addition, Alex, Elizabeth, and Daniel Pang, Craig and Diane Allen, and the entire history department made it possible for Heather to spend almost all of her time on this project this year and kept her from going crazy. For that they deserve more than thanks; they should receive some kind of medal.

The photographs in the book come from the Castilleja School Archive, which in turn acquired them from a myriad of sources, most now unknown or uncredited. We are grateful to all of the photographers over the years who left these treasures for us and to the people who put the photos in albums or wrote names under or on so many of the photos. In particular, we would like to thank photographers David Cardinal, Dawna Houston, Anne Dowie, Laura Ware Nethercut '79, David Renaud, and everyone who has ever taken a photo for *Paintbrush*.

We hope that this history becomes the starting point for a conversation about our past. Please visit the Castilleja web site (www.castilleja.org) to find ways to tell your Castilleja stories and enjoy other Castilleja memories as we celebrate the Castilleja Centennial.

ABOUT THE AUTHORS

Sara Croll graduated from Castilleja in 2005. She was editor-in-chief of *Paintbrush* and active in the drama program. She now attends Columbia University.

Heather Allen Pang graduated from Castilleja in 1984 and now teaches United States History to the eighth grade and serves as the Department Chair. Before returning to Castilleja in 1999, she earned her Ph. D. in American history at UC Davis, taught college, and worked as an editor for the Encyclopaedia Britannica web guide. She is also the school archivist.

Laura Arrillaga-Andreessen '88 supported the idea of this book from the beginning. Knowing that a school of Castilleja's excellence should celebrate its rich history, she recommended a substantial, visually pleasing book with serious content. Her enthusiasm for this project follows a long tradition of Arrillaga family support for educational institutions and initiatives. Inspired by her parents, John Arrillaga Sr. and the late Frances C. Arrillaga, Laura has earned her own reputation as a committed educator, social entrepreneur, and philanthropist, in addition to her continued involvement at Castilleja.